"Our school, The Gateway School of Mumbai, is in its first year of running its high school adaptive program and we have been working hard to figure out the best way to prepare our students for this transition to life, as young adults beyond school.... There is a lot of material on independent skills and transition programs out there, but the two things that made Francis's book invaluable to us were a) the organization of ideas into four essential themes, each with a concise but purposeful list of goals and activities, and b) the structured and explicit breakdown of the activities provided us novice teachers with the much-needed scaffolding that we were looking for as we implemented the program for the first time. Thank you, Francis, for compiling the knowledge accumulated through years of experience and study in this area, it has been an immense support to us!"

—**Radhika Zahedi, MA**, co-principal, The Gateway School of Mumbai

"This clear, complete, and practical skill-building guide will take young people all the way down the road to a successful transition to adult life. And it's a resource for family members, school staff, clinicians, and *anyone* who wants to help young people lead productive and satisfying lives. Don't think about transition without it."

—**Fredda Rosen**, executive director of Job Path, a New York City, NY-based not-for-profit that helps people with autism and other developmental disabilities find jobs, live in their own homes, and become part of community life

"*The ASD Independence Workbook* confronts the issues faced by young adults as they strive to be independent and assume their position in the community. Within each of the four content areas, the many tested and practical activities are presented in a rhythmic style that makes them easy to follow and understand. The book stands out because Tabone respects the competence of his readers and their desire to be a part of the majority culture without changing who they are. It will be a valuable resource in their quest to achieve a balanced and fulfilled life."

> —**Carole R. Gothelf, EdD**, director of individualized supports for AHRC New York City

"Working in special education for the last twenty years has made me realize how important these adaptive skills are to the independence and happiness of young people with ASD. This book is a much-needed resource for teachers and families, and can have a profound impact on the lives of young people with ASD if truly incorporated into their educational and transitional plans."

> —**Mark Lauterbach, PhD**, assistant professor for early childhood/art education; program head for special education at Brooklyn College

the asd independence workbook

transition skills for teens &
young adults with autism

FRANCIS TABONE, PhD

Instant Help Books
An Imprint of New Harbinger Publications, Inc.

Publisher's Note

This publication is designed to provide accurate and authoritative information in regard to the subject matter covered. It is sold with the understanding that the publisher is not engaged in rendering psychological, financial, legal, or other professional services. If expert assistance or counseling is needed, the services of a competent professional should be sought.

Distributed in Canada by Raincoast Books

Copyright © 2018 by Francis Tabone
           Instant Help Books
           An imprint of New Harbinger Publications, Inc.
           5674 Shattuck Avenue
           Oakland, CA 94609
           www.newharbinger.com

Cover design by Amy Shoup

Acquired by Jess O'Brien

Edited by Karen Schader

Library of Congress Cataloging-in-Publication Data on file

Printed in the United States of America.

23   22   21

10   9   8   7   6   5   4   3   2

contents

Part 3: Leisure Time

Part 4: Community Use

Independence. What a beautiful word. For the parents of ASD kids, it's the word we dream about—but also the one that keeps us up at night. How, we wonder, can we have such wonderful, talented kids, sometimes with extraordinary skills, who often find the simplest tasks so daunting?

Every day I look at my own son, Gus, and think: *What the hell. You can play the piano so beautifully. Why can't you slice an apple? Why can't you shave without mowing one of your eyebrows off?* And more importantly: *Will you ever learn that not everyone wants to discuss the New York City transit system with you?*

Well, Francis Tabone has written this book for my kid, and for yours, and for you. Entertaining and thoughtful, *The ASD Independence Workbook* is exactly what it says it is: a step-by-step instruction manual that breaks down everyday tasks and situations—the ones ASD kids find so challenging—into skills that can be practiced and mastered.

Whether the issue is hygiene, proper ways to start a conversation, or safety on the Internet, Dr. Tabone Explains It All For You. It won't be easy—let's face it, practicing life skills with your child can make you want to throw the book, or the child, against the wall. Because what takes a neurotypical kid three repetitions to master may take an ASD kid a hundred repetitions. Or a thousand. *But master it they do.*

At Cooke Academy, where Dr. Tabone is the principal and my son is a student, this workbook is an essential part of the curriculum. My son's latest favorite expression is "Ohh, *now* I get it." This doesn't necessarily mean he will now do whatever I'm asking, or change his behavior right away. But it means that the tiny cartoon lightbulb over his head is actually switched on. *He gets it.* Now: practice, practice practice.

Like so many things about Gus, I cherish his naivete at the same time that I know how it keeps him dependent on me. It's that literal-mindedness, the inability to see other people's motives—or indeed that other people *have* motives—that is both endearing and concerning. We have been using the exercises in *The ASD Independence Workbook* to discuss and change some of his interpersonal habits—so that, for example, Gus does not empty his pockets every time a homeless person asks him for money.

And sometimes practicing these small changes of behavior leads to bigger realizations. I have talked and talked and talked about not just giving private information to anyone who asks. And yesterday, Gus showed me a number that appeared on his telephone that he did not recognize. "Mom, that is probably a telemarketer," he said. Then, there was the pause for thought. "There are people in the world," he said slowly, "who are not always good." Apologies to telemarketers, but with that one sentence, my sixteen-year-old son came incrementally closer to being able to function independently. (Now if I can only get him to shave….)

Work this workbook. If you are a young adult on the spectrum, it will be a guide to refer to when a social interaction or conversation confuses you. And if you are the parent or caregiver of someone with ASD, it will help you help him stand proudly on his own. And that is the ultimate gift of love.

    —Judith Newman
        Author, *To Siri with Love: A Mother, Her Autistic Son, and the Kindness of Machines*

introduction

Dear Reader,

All students in high school make plans for what happens after. Many students work with teachers, guidance counselors, family, and even friends to help prepare them for life after high school. Leaving high school is exciting and challenging at the same time. Many things will be different, which can often mean having to learn new routines and meeting new people, and that may present new challenges. But there will also be new experiences that you may enjoy and the opportunity to focus on new skills and activities that can greatly enhance your life. As the reader of this book, it is important to practice the things you learned in school and use those skills in your day-to-day life. In this way, you can meet new experiences with more confidence and find joy and excitement in your adult life.

In high school, you probably heard the word "transition." You may have even attended meetings with school personnel and parents to do some transition planning. While the idea of transition is simple, the planning and organization of your transition to post–high school life may be complex. There are lots of things to remember that you learned in school. Hopefully the activities and lessons in this book will help you remember that work and give you a chance to practice while you use these skills during your daily routines.

These transition skills are broken into four parts that are most important to your daily living. You will work on activities that highlight communication skills; health, hygiene, and safety skills; developing leisure activities; and using community resources. Each section will give you a chance to practice how to best support your independence and growth in this area. Some of the activities are available for download at the website for this book: http://www.newharbinger.com/40644. (See the last page of this book for details.)

You can work with a clinician or parent on activities, or you can work by yourself. It is always a good idea to get feedback if you are working on your own to make sure your work reflects the ideas that will give you greater independence and successful entry into the world as an adult.

Some activities may prove challenging; others may help remind you of the life skills you have learned during your school years. Remember to simply try your best. If anything is too challenging, ask for help! Asking for help is an important skill to use as you work through these activities. Another important skill is being flexible. Being flexible includes taking advice and criticism from others. It will help make your progress that much better on your road to independence.

Part 1
Communication Skills

Every day we communicate with many people. We talk, use our bodies, and use social cues to help us ask for information and receive information as well. We talk to our friends and families so we can share our experiences and understand others. The better your communication skills, the more success you will find at work, with friends, and in your day-to-day routines.

It is important that we follow certain rules when we communicate. For example, we need to be good listeners. We need to answer the questions that are posed to us. We need to make sure that people understand us, and that we understand them equally. Developing good friendships and relationships means you have to listen as well as communicate effectively. This cannot happen unless your communication skills show that you enjoy both listening and talking with others. Having interest in others will help them be more interested in what you have to say. No one likes a one-sided relationship, where one person does the talking and the other doesn't get a chance to share his or her interests. In addition, others can get frustrated if they feel you are not listening.

Many times you may want to talk about a topic that is interesting to you. You may even feel like everyone else would be interested as well. This is not always the case. We need to understand that what is interesting to you may not be interesting to others. You cannot always talk about what you want, because others also have interests and ideas that they feel are important. If you ignore the ideas of others, you may find people are less likely to talk to you or want to spend time with you. They may feel that they won't have a chance to talk or share their ideas.

The urge to talk about your topic may be strong, but in certain situations it is not always appropriate. For example, if someone asks you a question, you need to make sure that you're answering the questions and not introducing your own topic. Equally, a friend or family member may want to start a conversation. This means you need to listen for the topic and reply with a statement that is on-topic, not introduce a different topic. This can be difficult at times.

When speaking to others, using a clear voice, using appropriate body language, and listening are all important. You want your words to be understood. To do so, it is important to use clear, concise language. In this way, you will make yourself heard and are more likely to get answers to your questions.

The activities in this section will help you remember the rules of conversation. They will help you do your best in any situation that requires interaction with others. It is always important that you understand others and that you're understood as well.

identifying the topic 1

---

you need to know

It is important to be a good listener so you know what a person is talking about. Listen carefully to understand the main idea or the topic that person is focused on. When you understand the topic, you can then respond with an on-topic response and engage in a conversation. Listening carefully is the first step to encouraging good relationships with others. If you don't, the speaker may feel insulted or annoyed.

Let's start with some activities that will help us identify the topic:

Bill and Jim are walking to school. Jim says, "My brother is home from college. I am excited to see him because he has been away for a long time. We are going to have a welcome-home party for him. My brother is almost finished with his first year in school. When he is finished, he will move back home."

What was the topic in this example? Was it about a welcome-home party? Not really. That was part of what Jim said, but what was the main idea? If you figured out that the topic of Jim's statement was his brother, you are correct. Jim gave us lots of information about his brother, so we would say the topic was Jim's brother.

We could ask lots of questions like, "Where does he go to school?" or "Who is going to the party for your brother?" It would be a polite way to acknowledge that you are listening to the speaker. We should respond to the speaker with question like these, so that the speaker knows we are listening and are interested in what he is saying. Responding off-topic could hurt the speaker's feeling or give him the sense you really don't care about what he is saying.

directions

Read each statement carefully. Think about the main idea, or topic, of the statement. Then write down the topic of each statement using one or two words.

1. Jim asked, "Hi. Did you watch the news this morning? They say there is going to be a big rainstorm coming."

   Topic? _____

2. Bill said, "I thought the homework last night was really difficult. It took me almost two hours to finish. By the time I was done, I was ready for bed."

   Topic? _____

3. Edward stated, "Once I went to a Chinese restaurant downtown and had an amazing meal. I had dumplings that were filled with a delicious mix of vegetables. There was a dipping sauce that was terrific!"

   Topic? _____

4. Ryan said, "I love video games. My favorites are car-racing games. There is a new one coming out next month, and I will definitely buy a copy."

   Topic? _____

5. Ella asked, "Is anyone going to the dance on Friday night? I think it will be fun. I really want to go but don't want to go alone."

   Topic? _____

6. Debbie said, "I am having trouble deciding on which movie to go to. One is an action film, the other is a comedy. I want to see both but only have time for one."

   Topic? _____

7. Lacey replied, "I was late for school. I couldn't get out of bed. I need to go to sleep earlier."

   Topic? _____

8. Arlen said, "The restroom is a real mess. Someone needs to get in there and clean it up."

   Topic? _____

9. Wendy shouted, "Someone ate my lunch! Whoever did it better buy me a new one!"

   Topic? _____

10. Joanna stated, "My teachers are the best. I have learned so much. I really love them all."

    Topic? _____

take note

Write a few sentences about the kinds of topics you enjoy talking about with friends and family.

_____

_____

_____

_____

Are there times that others ignore you or do not want to have a conversation about your topics?

_____

_____

_____

How do you feel when someone changes the topic or ignores what you are saying?

_____

_____

_____

What would you say to someone who changes the topic or ignores what you are saying?

_____

_____

_____

Is there someone you always enjoy talking with? What are the usual topics you discuss?

_____

_____

_____

2 knowing the difference between on-topic and off-topic

Jim and Bill are walking to school. Jim says to Bill, "I was not able to finish my homework last night. I got home late and had to get to sleep. I sure hope the teacher understands." Bill responds to Jim and says, "I am sure the teacher will understand. She usually allows students to make up work when they cannot finish in time."

In this example, did Bill stay on-topic? Yes, he did. Let's look at why. Jim is talking about missing homework and wondering how his teacher will respond. Bill answers with something related. Bill reassures his friend that the teacher usually understands these situations and allows students to make up work. Bill's answer is directly connected to what Jim said.

Jim and Bill are walking to school. Jim says to Bill, "I was not able to finish my homework last night. I got home late and had to get to sleep. I sure hope the teacher understands." Bill responds to Jim and says, "I want to have pizza for lunch today."

In this example, did Bill stay on-topic? No, he did not. Let's look at why. Jim is talking about missing homework and wondering how his teacher will respond. Bill answers with something that has nothing to do with school or missing homework. Think about how Jim might feel when Bill replied with an off-topic statement. Was Bill being polite?

directions

Carefully read each conversation. Decide whether the second speaker was on-topic or off-topic. Circle the answer that best fits the response.

Jim: "What are you having for lunch today? I am going to the corner to buy pizza. Do you want to join me?"

Bill: "Yes, I would love to go with you."

Bill was   on-topic   off-topic

Jenn: "Today is my brother's birthday, and I have to get him a present. He likes to read, so I thought I would get him a book. I am having trouble picking something he would like to read. I know he likes science fiction, so maybe I can find something at the bookstore that he does not already have."

David: "For my birthday, I got a collection of science fiction stories. Maybe he would like that."

David was   on-topic   off-topic

Amy: "I finished my work early so I was able to watch a little television. I watched the news. What do you do when you finish work early?"

Chloe: "I am hungry and I want to eat right now."

Chloe was   on-topic   off-topic

Yumi: "The dance is on Friday, and I have to get a new dress. I am not sure what color would be best, but I will look around at the store. What will you wear to the dance?"

Ryan: "Did you see the new Star Wars movie?"

      Ryan was   on-topic   off-topic

_____

Juan: "Does the train to Ninety-Sixth Street stop at this station?"

Kelvin: "No, it doesn't. This train goes downtown. You will need to take an uptown train."

      Kelvin was   on-topic   off-topic

_____

Ginny: "Is that your book on the table? If it is, please put it away."

Robert: "It is a book about zebras. Zebras are my favorite animals."

      Robert was   on-topic   off-topic

_____

Kaleb: "I am going to take my dog for a walk. Do you want to come with me? We can stop at the store for a snack."

Connie: "I do not like dogs. I got bitten by a dog when I was little and got five stitches."

      Connie was   on-topic   off-topic

_____

Ludi: "Is there any way I can borrow your book tonight? I left mine at work and want to catch up on the reading."

Emily: "No, because I need to work on it tonight as well."

Emily was   on-topic   off-topic

take note

Looking back at the examples from this activity, was it hard or easy to identify whether the speaker was on- or off-topic? What clues or words helped you to identify on- or off-topic statements?

_____

_____

_____

If someone is asking you a question or discussing something and you do not understand, how does it make you feel?

_____

_____

_____

Write a sentence or two on how you would respond to someone who was talking about a topic you did not understand.

_____

_____

_____

Write a sentence or two on how you would respond if you were not interested in a topic someone brought up in a conversation.

_____

_____

_____

Why is it important to use polite language when you don't want to talk about a particular topic?

_____

_____

_____

appropriate conversation starters 3

---

you need to know

Make sure you are answering a question or comment with the same topic as the speaker. When someone talks to you, it is not polite to change the subject without acknowledging the speaker. It is okay to say that the topic is not something you are really interested in, but it needs to be done politely, not by immediately changing the subject. To build a good friendship, you must be ready to listen to others and respond to their statements.

Elana was speaking with her brother at the dinner table. She said, "I was so happy today I got 100 percent on my spelling test. I was so proud of myself because I really studied. Spelling is not my best subject, so I am really proud of myself. I think I did a great job."

Her brother Peter replied, "Tomorrow is Wednesday. Every Wednesday we have gym, so I need to remember my sneakers. If I forget, I have to sit on the side, and I do not want to sit on the side."

"Peter," Elana shouted, "didn't you hear what I said! Why don't you ever listen to me? I was telling you about my spelling test, and you didn't even listen."

It probably would have been better if Peter mentioned something about his sister's success on the spelling test. Simply saying "You did a great job" or "I am proud of you" would have shown that Peter was listening. How do you think Elana felt after her brother replied? Do you think her feelings were hurt? What would a better response have been?

Good conversations require good listening. You have to be flexible and often talk about things that might not be on your mind at the moment. Conversations that are back and forth and that stay on-topic will help develop friendships and maintain a good experience for both people. Changing a topic or giving an answer that is off-topic may be seen as rude; it may seem as though you are not listening.

directions

After each of these conversation starters, write a response that would be on-topic.

Jim: "Hi. Did you watch the news this morning? They say there is going to be a big rainstorm coming."

Your response: _____

_____

Bill: "I thought the homework last night was really difficult. It took me almost two hours to finish. By the time I was done, I was ready for bed."

Your response: _____

_____

Yumi: "I really want a new dress for the dance on Friday. I'm just not sure what color to get."

Your response: _____

_____

Ryan: "I love video games. My favorites are car-racing games. There is a new one coming out next month, and I will definitely buy a copy."

Your response: _____

_____

Juan: "Does the train to Ninety-Sixth Street stop at this station?"

Your response: _____

_____

take note

Sometimes it is difficult to begin a conversation with someone. A good idea is to list all the topics you are interested in so that when you meet someone you have lots of things to talk about. Let's make a list of topics that you are interested in. Then list two people you can have a conversation with about each topic.

Topic: _____

People I can talk to about this topic:

- _____

- _____

Topic: _____

People I can talk to about this topic:

- _____

- _____

Topic: _____

People I can talk to about this topic:

- _____

- _____

4   asking for help

you need to know

When you need help finding solutions to a problem, you can ask for it. Asking someone for help is something we do every day in many situations. Sometimes it's easy to recognize that you need help—for example, when you're trying to open a stuck jar. Some situations where you need help are less obvious. If you are walking to an appointment, and it is taking longer than usual and you don't recognize where you are, you may be lost and need to ask for help in finding your way. Being independent doesn't mean you have to do everything on your own; asking for help when you need it in your daily routines is also part of being independent. Knowing who and when to ask for help is tricky, but we can look at ways to identify good times to ask for help.

Michelle was in the drugstore looking for aspirin. She checked aisle after aisle and could not find what she was looking for. She went through each product carefully but still could not find the aspirin. After thirty minutes of looking, she left and went to a different drugstore. This time, when she began to look for the aspirin, a clerk from the store asked, "Can I help you find something?"

Michelle responded, "I am looking for aspirin."

"No problem. It is in aisle 3; follow me," the clerk responded. The clerk brought her to the location and showed her the item. Michelle thanked the clerk, paid at the cashier, and left.

Michelle could have saved a lot of time in the first store if she had asked a clerk for help. She was lucky in the second store because the clerk approached her to see if she needed help. This will not always happen. It is important to seek help from someone when you feel you are not able to solve a problem on your own.

directions

On the lines below, make a list of daily routines you can do well on your own.

_____

_____

_____

_____

Now, make a list of routines you may have needed help with in the past. Next to each, identify a person who can help you with each routine you identified in the second column.

Routine you may have needed help with in the past	Who can help you with this routine?

Next, let's look at these stories and see if we can help the characters ask for help.

Julie is at the train station but cannot find the track her train is leaving from. If she waits too long, she will miss her train. Another train going to her station does not leave until the next day. She checks each track but cannot find her train.

Who can Julie ask for help?

_____

_____

What could she ask to get the information she needs?

"_____

_____"

Larry is making a project in his art class. He tries hard to find the blue paint he needs to finish his work, but it is nowhere on the shelf of paints. He is very concerned that his painting will not come out the way he wants without the color blue. He is getting very upset.

Who can Larry ask for help?

_____

_____

What could he ask to get the information he needs?

"_____

_____"

take note

Think about a time you needed help and asked for it. How did the situation work out?

_____

_____

_____

_____

How did you feel asking for help?

_____

_____

_____

How do you usually feel after receiving help?

_____

_____

Why might you not ask for help even when you need it?

_____

_____

_____

5   requesting items

you need to know

If you are in a store, at a restaurant, at the movies, or even at home, you will communicate your needs by asking for something. Doing so requires a few things to remember. First, you must use a clear voice. You can't whisper or mumble, or you may not be understood. You also need to use full sentences. Pointing or simply using one word is not going to get you what you need. And finally, be polite. Using words like "please" and "thank you" will make the experience much easier and personal for both you and the person you are requesting an item from. When you follow these instructions, people will understand your needs and be ready to help.

Marcos was at the store and needed to buy a notebook. When the clerk asked if he needed help, Marcos did not say anything. He pointed to a shelf with notebooks. The clerk asked if he needed a notebook, and Marcos whispered yes. The clerk asked which one, and Marcos simply pointed to the stacks of notebooks. The clerk asked, "How about this one?" Marcos did not answer but just nodded. Marcos paid for the notebook. When he got home, his tutor said, "This is not the type of notebook you need."

Marcos should have told the clerk he needed a certain type of notebook. He also could have written it down to help remember. He did not answer the clerk's questions in full sentences, nor did he ask questions.

Always remember to

1. Use a clear voice.

    • People cannot help if you don't speak up.

2. Use a full sentence.

    • Without proper language, people will not understand your need.

3. Use "please" and "thank you."

    • Being polite will always encourage others to help you

directions

Use these scenarios to role-play or act out a scene with a partner. Remember that when you are requesting an item you use a clear voice, full sentences, and polite words.

1. You are in a restaurant. You would like to order a meal and a drink. What would you say to the waiter when he asks to take your order?

2. You are shopping for a shirt. What information do you need to tell the clerk? What details does the clerk need to help you find what you are looking for?

3. You are at the library looking for a book on George Washington. How would you ask the librarian for help?

Take a look at these requests. Using full sentences, rewrite each so that it forms a clear, polite request.

1. I need a pencil.

   _____

2. Give me the soda.

   _____

3. Get me my coat.

   _____

4. I cannot find the shampoo.

   _____

5. Where is my book bag?

   _____

6. I want that seat.

   _____

7. Let me have that bag.

   _____

take note

Remember, when making a request, it is important to use a clear voice, full sentences, and polite words.

Why is it important to use a clear voice when making a request?

_____

_____

_____

_____

Why is it important to use full sentences?

_____

_____

_____

_____

Why is it important to use polite words?

_____

_____

_____

_____

6   asking clarifying questions

you need to know

Asking questions is a good thing! When we receive instructions or directions, we sometimes need to ask a clarifying question so that we know we have all the information to carry out an activity. To know if we have all the information we need, it is useful to use the five Ws: who, what, where, when, and why. The five Ws give us a way to gather information, and then we can evaluate whether we have all the information we need. For example, if you had a doctor's appointment tomorrow at 8:00 a.m., what else would you need to know? You would need to know where the office is, and you would need to know why you were going to make sure you had all the information to bring to the doctor. Asking clarifying questions will help make directions clearer so you can be successful at whatever task you are doing. Without them you won't have all the information to help you succeed in everyday tasks.

Martha received an email inviting her to Chloe's birthday celebration. It read, "Join me at Joe's Restaurant, 20 Main Street, on Saturday. I am looking forward to spending my birthday with you!" Martha was excited for the lunch celebration, and at noon on Saturday, she got dressed and headed to the restaurant. When she got there, the waiter told her that her party did not start until 8:00 p.m. That was a full eight hours later! Martha went back home and waited until it was time to go back to the party.

So Martha wasted a trip because she did not have enough information. What clarifying question should she have asked? Let's use the five Ws to see what information was missing.

Who? Chloe

What? A dinner birthday celebration

Where? Joe's Restaurant, 20 Main Street

When? Saturday

Why? To celebrate Chloe's birthday

What is missing? We know exactly who is throwing the party. We know exactly where the party is. Do we know when it begins? We know only that it is on Saturday. Chloe forgot to include the time. Martha could have saved herself a trip if she asked the clarifying question, "What time does the party start?"

directions

Take a look at these scenarios. Use the five Ws to help decide if you have enough information or need to ask a clarifying question.

Juan called Rachel to ask her to a movie. Juan said, "There is a new movie playing. Want to go tonight? There is a show at eight o'clock. I can meet you a few minutes early so we can buy tickets." Rachel asked, "Great! What is the name of the movie?" Juan said, "It is called *A Love Story*." "Okay," said Rachel. "I will meet you later." Later that night, both were waiting at different theaters.

Who? _____ What? _____ Where? _____

When? _____ Why? _____

Write a clarifying question Rachel should have asked.

_____

_____

Sam's sister gives him an envelope to bring to his school. "This is important," she said. "Don't forget to hand this in." When Sam went to school the next day he remembered the envelope, but he did not know who to give it to.

Who? _____ What? _____ Where? _____

When? _____ Why? _____

Write a clarifying question Sam should have asked.

_____

_____

Tamara called her doctor's office and made an appointment for Tuesday, March 11, at eight o'clock in the morning. The receptionist told her that the office had moved to a new location. Tamara asked, "What documents do I need to bring for my checkup?" The receptionist replied, "Please bring your insurance card." "Thank you," Tamara said, and hung up the phone.

Who? _____ What? _____ Where? _____

When? _____ Why? _____

Write a clarifying question Tamara should have asked.

_____

_____

take note

Think about a time when you didn't have enough information to solve a problem or carry out a task. What clarifying question could you have asked to help you gain more information?

_____

_____

_____

_____

Think about a time you helped someone get something done. What questions did they ask?

_____

_____

_____

_____

What happens when you don't have enough information?

_____

_____

_____

_____

Who can you go to for help at home, at school, and at your agency?

_____

_____

_____

_____

idiomatic speech 7

---

you need to know

Idioms are a part of language that may seem confusing. Basically, an idiom is an expression that doesn't mean exactly what it says. For example, you may have heard the term "a fish out of water" and wondered what that meant. It doesn't mean that a fish is out of water; it means that something or someone is in an unusual space. If you were in a new situation and didn't know what to do, you might say, "I feel like a fish out of water." We use idioms all the time to express a mood or a feeling. You are not supposed to interpret these words literally; rather, you need to see them as a symbol or metaphor for something else.

Ellen asked Judy, "A penny for your thoughts?"

Judy looked at Ellen and didn't understand what she was saying. Ellen said again, "A penny for your thoughts? It means, "What are you thinking?" "Oh," said Judy, "I was thinking about asking my supervisor for a raise."

Ellen said, "Well, you are barking up the wrong tree."

Judy looked at Ellen again and said, "What do you mean?" Ellen repeated, "You are barking up the wrong tree. It means you are looking in the wrong place; you are asking the wrong person. You have to go to the owner, not the supervisor, for a raise. Today is a good day to ask for a raise. I heard it through the grapevine that the owner is in a good mood."

"Grapevine?" said Judy. "What grapevine?" Ellen smiled. "It is an expression. It means I heard rumors from a few people."

"Well, then," said Judy, "I am off to ask for a raise."

Ellen uses idioms to highlight her points. But if you don't know the idioms, you may find it confusing.

directions

The column on the left is a list of common idioms. The column on the right explains what those idioms mean. Draw a line from left to right to connect an idiom with its actual meaning. Ask for help if needed.

1. It is a piece of cake	a.	To do something in the easiest, cheapest, or quickest way
2. Break a leg	b.	Feel sick
3. To cut corners	c.	Something will never happen
4. Hit the nail on the head	d.	Good luck (often used by actors before going onstage)
5. Feel under the weather	e.	An issue left unaddressed because of its sensitive nature
6. Don't judge a book by its cover	f.	Harassing or bothering someone
7. When pigs fly	g.	Something is easy
8. See eye to eye	h.	During good and bad times
9. The elephant in the room	i.	Get something correct
10. Busting chops	j.	Bad weather
11. Raining cats and dogs	k.	What you do is more important than what you say
12. All ears	l.	Don't judge something by the way it looks
13. Actions speak louder than words	m.	Agree on something
14. Through thick and thin	n.	Listening carefully

Answer Key: 1 g, 2 d, 3 a, 4 i, 5 b, 6 l, 7 c, 8 m, 9 e, 10 f, 11 j, 12 n, k 13, 14 h

How could you rewrite these sentences so that they do not use idioms?

My brother and I don't always see eye to eye.

_____

I am going to call in sick because I feel under the weather.

_____

I will call her when pigs fly.

_____

See you tonight on the stage. Break a leg!

_____

I think she will be a good president; her actions speak louder than words.

_____

You hit the nail right on the head. I completely agree with you!

_____

Learning to ride a bicycle was a piece of cake for me.

_____

If you are looking for me to help, you are barking up the wrong tree.

_____

Try this food. It is good, so don't judge a book by its cover.

_____

I am going catch some Zs.

_____

take note

What is an idiom?

_____

_____

_____

Why would people use this type of language?

_____

_____

_____

What other examples of idioms that were not part of this activity can you think of?

_____

_____

_____

What are some clues that would let you know someone is using idiomatic speech?

_____

_____

_____

8 entering and exiting a conversation

you need to know

A conversation has at least two people: you and another person. When entering and exiting a conversation, it is important to follow several rules. First of all, if you are going to join a conversation that is already going on, you will need to know the topic being discussed. Joining a conversation and introducing a new topic can be seen as rude, or an interruption, so be mindful of knowing what others are talking about.

If you are finished with a conversation, you need to let the other person know by saying something like, "Okay, see you later." Just walking away abruptly may seem like you left in the middle of the conversation. That may seem rude to the other person.

Mario and Jenn were talking about their afterschool program. Dennis came over and said, "I was walking to school today and I saw a fire truck." Mario said, "Dude, that is rude. We were having a conversation."

* * *

Horace and Frank were talking about the new action movie they had seen. Horace said, "My favorite part was when the hero saves the hostages." Frank said, "I liked it when the hero captured the bad guy." Horace walked away. Frank thought, "Is he mad at me?"

* * *

Willis and Stephen were talking about their favorite restaurants. Jamie came over and said, "Hey guys, what's up?" Willis said, "I was just telling Stephen that I love the new restaurant that opened on Main Street." Stephen said, "Yes, I really want to try it." Jamie said, "I heard it was great. I was planning to go this weekend." "Cool," said Willis. "Let me know how it is." Jamie said, "I will. Okay, I have to run to work. See you later."

Only one of those examples shows the correct way to enter and exit a conversation. The first example shows how it can be a problem to enter a conversation without respecting what the topic is and trying to change it abruptly. It was perceived as rude. The second conversation shows what happens if you simply walk away without finishing a conversation. It was perceived as being angry. Just like a phone call, we always say good-bye before we hang up so the other person knows we are finished.

directions

Write a sentence showing how you might enter or exit a conversation given the details of the situation. Remember, being polite will make others feel good and will encourage further conversations.

At the lunch table Juan and Jeff are talking about a television show. How would you join the conversation?

_____

_____

_____

When it is time to go back to work, how would you leave the conversation with Juan and Jeff?

_____

_____

_____

Lisa and Natalia are talking about an upcoming wedding. You are anxious to share some news with them. What would you say when entering the conversation?

_____

_____

_____

After delivering your news, how would you leave the conversation?

_____

_____

_____

take note

What are some appropriate phrases you could use to enter a conversation where two people are talking?

_____

_____

_____

_____

How would others know that you are finished talking with them? What would you say?

_____

_____

_____

_____

How would people respond if you walked into a conversation without acknowledging their topic and started talking about something else?

_____

_____

_____

_____

How might people react if you were having a conversation and you walked away without ending the conversation?

_____

_____

_____

_____

9   body language

you need to know

Body language is what your body says not by talking but by its position and your movements. For example, if someone is talking to you and you are looking out the window, your body may be saying, "I am not paying attention." What about when you fold your arms and keep your head down when someone is talking to you? That may seem like you are angry or do not want to stand and talk.

There are a few essential rules about your posture, eye contact, and movements during a conversation. You should always be facing the speaker, with your eyes looking at the person who is talking. Your arms and legs should be still, and you should be standing an arm's length away from the person. Standing too close or too far can be uncomfortable for the person you are speaking with. Keeping a calm body is important as well. To minimize distractions, try not to move or rock while talking. It may take some focus but it will make your conversation more efficient.

Sam was talking to his teacher. His head was down, and he was looking away from her. His body was at least three arms' lengths away from the teacher. As she approached, Sam moved back. Sam was also twirling his fingers. The teacher repeatedly instructed Sam to look up and pay attention. Sam had a hard time doing so.

When they have conversations, some people form barriers by crossing their arms or legs, or holding something that blocks them from the other person. Their bodies are closed. Try to keep your body open. When sitting, lean forward. If you lean forward, you are more visible to other people at the table and it is easier to converse with them. Leaning backward, away from the other person, may seem like disinterest.

It isn't always easy to keep focused on maintaining body language and paying attention at the same time. All you can do is your best. If you are having trouble with body language, it is okay to use words to tell others that you are listening to them.

directions

When you are having a conversation, your body language (the way your body is positioned) is important. For each part of the diagram, explain how and where the body parts should be during a conversation. Think about what a good listener looks like during a conversation.

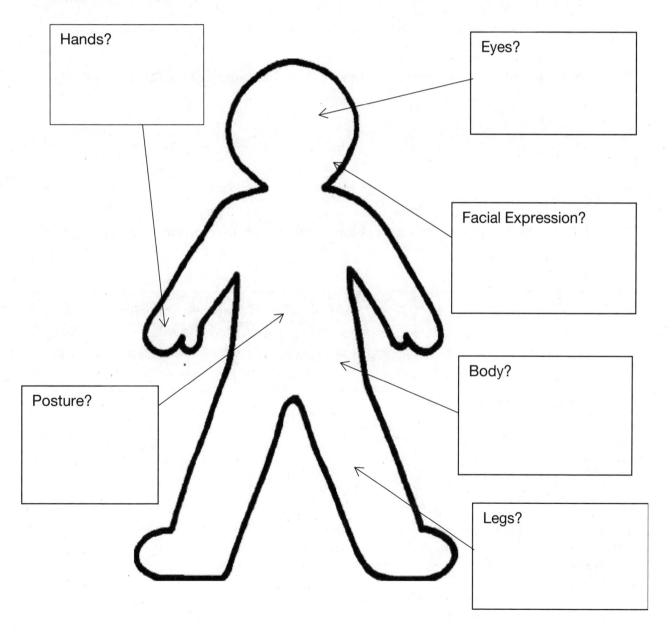

Hands?

Eyes?

Facial Expression?

Posture?

Body?

Legs?

take note

Think about times when you are having a conversation with someone. What elements of body language might be difficult for you?

_____

_____

You are having a conversation with someone, but maintaining eye contact is difficult. What could you say to let the other person know you are listening?

_____

_____

For each area, check off how difficult it is for you to maintain appropriate body language.

	Easy to show appropriate body language	Not that difficult to show appropriate body language	Hard to show appropriate body language
Eyes			
Hands			
Facial expression			
Standing comfortable distance			
Legs			
Posture			

posture for effective communication 10

---

you need to know

Let's take a closer look at how posture is part of communication. Your posture can tell other that you are receptive to their conversation. We call this open posture. Some posture tells others that you are not receptive to their conversation. This is called closed posture.

What does open posture look like? You are facing the person with your hands apart, or perhaps on the arms of a chair. You are leaning forward and looking at the person. Closed posture is the opposite. Your hands are folded; your legs may be crossed. You are leaning away from rather than toward the person. Your eyes are not focused on the speaker.

A helpful way to remember best posture during a conversation is to use the concept of mirroring. Mirroring is when you copy the posture of the person who is speaking to you. Look at the other person's arms and face and then take note of your body. Are they the same?

Melissa and David were at work. Melissa was speaking to David about the task they needed to complete. Melissa's body was an arm's length away from David. She had her arms at her sides, and she was looking directly at David. David had his arms crossed, and he was holding his shoulders. He was unable to look directly at Melissa. Melissa said, "David, I need to know you are listening to me." David remembered to use mirroring to help maintain appropriate body language. He positioned his arms the same as Melissa's and kept his head and gaze facing her.

In this case, David used the mirroring strategy to help him maintain appropriate body language, which created an open communication. Both parties used their bodies to communicate that they were indeed listening to each other. When David followed Melissa's body language, Melissa knew he was participating. It made her feel much better to know that David understood what was going on. Your body language can sometimes be as important as your words, so try to remember to mirror the speaker if you are having difficulty.

directions

1. Stand in front of the mirror. Take a look at how you are standing. Notice whether you are presenting open or closed body language.

2. Make an open posture. Describe the things that are important in presenting your body language as being open.

   _____

   _____

3. Now imitate what closed posture looks like.

4. Think about the difference between open and closed posture. Notice how you feel on the inside as well. Which one feels more comfortable: open or closed? Why?

   _____

   _____

   _____

   _____

5. Which position feels like it would be easier to use when having a conversation?

    _____

6. Your boss is speaking with you. What type of posture would you have? Describe
    what that would look like.

    _____

    _____

    _____

    _____

take note

Open posture communicates to others:

- You are listening.

- You are receptive to what they are saying.

- You are interested in what they say.

- You care about what they say.

- They are being heard.

Closed posture communicates to others:

- You may not be listening.

- You are not receptive to what they are saying.

- You are not interested in what they say.

- You may not care about what they say.

- They are not being heard.

Use open posture when having a conversation to communicate to others that you are interested and engaged. It is important to maintain good social skills and be courteous to those you will interact with in the community.

Part 2

Health, Hygiene, and Safety

Keeping yourself safe and healthy requires planning and organization. In this part, you will learn about a few tools to help take care of daily health and hygiene routines, organize checkups and doctor appointments, and make sure your living environment is safe.

What is the starting point to maintaining a healthy and safe lifestyle? Probably making sure to eat the right foods and maintaining a healthy diet. For example, you may like pizza. But eating pizza every day is not a healthy thing to do. Limiting yourself to only a few types of foods can lead to serious health issues.

Lots of times we just move through the day following routines and activities we are used to. You may have to cross a street to get where you are going. If you do it every day, you may forget to look both ways, pay attention to traffic signals, or use walkways. Sometimes when we do things over and over we act on impulse and forget the sequence of steps needed to keep us safe.

Tools like checklists and journals are a way to help remind you of what is needed on a day-to-day basis. For example, a food journal can help remind you of your eating habits. If you see that you've eaten pizza for four days in a row, perhaps it is time for something healthier. Even just listing the fruits and vegetables you eat every day can show you how well you are doing maintaining a healthy diet.

Hygiene is essential for maintaining relationships and keeping your appearance in the workplace appropriate, and it will affect your health. Building strong self-care routines will help you present your best look—fresh breath, a clean appearance, and neat clothing are all social norms we are expected to keep to as we navigate the community. Maintaining good hygiene will strengthen your relationships and is necessary for employment.

Cause and effect is another important element you will read about in this part. You will be able to clearly see how safe decision making and all the choices we make regarding our health will have an effect on our lives. Eating too much junk food (cause) may lead to weight gain or feeling sick (effect). Sharing personal information over the Internet (cause) may lead to identity theft, fraudulent charges on a credit card, or even worse (effect). You have to make decisions that will have a positive effect on your health and well-being.

you need to know

Leaving the house and forgetting to brush your teeth could be a problem. Bad breath is surely a way to keep people away from you! Something as simple as putting all your hygiene supplies in one place is a great way to remember all the steps you will need to go through in the morning before you leave your home. Things like a toothbrush, toothpaste, deodorant, and other hygiene supplies can be purchased in advance and placed in a small case or ziplock bag and kept in your bathroom. This way, you know you have everything you need. But how do you know what goes in there? There are hundreds of products for sale. Finding the right things can be tough without using a tool to help get you through the aisles at a drugstore.

Carmen needs to shop for supplies for her hygiene kit. When she arrives at the store, she is overwhelmed by the number of products in the store. In addition, there are hundreds of items she doesn't know the use for. Fortunately, she has brought along her morning-mirror checklist. It has all the steps she needs to find the exact items she needs. In addition, her caregiver gave her additional items to look for.

Looking over her checklist, Carmen sees that brushing her teeth is first, so she finds a toothbrush and toothpaste. She will need a hairbrush next. Then she needs to find deodorant. Her caregiver has written that she also needs eye drops, aspirin, hair bands, and feminine products such as tampons or sanitary napkins. She is not sure what all these products are for, so when she gets home she and her caregiver sit down and make a list of the items she purchased. They use a Who, What, Where, When, and Why chart and go through each item. First she picked out the deodorant and filled in the chart.

Item	Who (men, women, or everyone?)	What	Where	When	Why
Deodorant	Everyone	Deodorant (You may list the brand name as well.)	In the bathroom or locker room	After I shower and after I go to the gym	Helps with sweating and odor

Carmen did this for every item, and it helped her understand all the details of her purchase. In this way, she was always prepared to take care of her hygiene needs.

directions

Make a list of products you will need to create a hygiene kit. Ask a parent or caregiver to help think about your needs and routines every morning. Think about things that you can put into the kit that will help your morning routine go quickly and easily.

Items for My Hygiene Kit

1.	2.	3.	4.	5.
6.	7.	8.	9.	10.

Copy the items into the following chart. Then, for every item on your list, add the who, what, where, when, and why. For who, you can think about groups of people, like women or men. At http://www.newharbinger.com/40644, you can download a form to use for your chart.

Item	Who uses the product?	What is this product used for?	Where do you use the product?	When do you use the product?	Why do you use this product?

take note

What other type of kit could be helpful? Maybe a first-aid kit? Or a medical kit that holds all medications you may need to take on a daily basis?

How might one of these kits be helpful to your daily routine?

_____

_____

_____

What kinds of kits would be useful to you?

_____

Let's begin to put one of these kits together. What kind of kit will you make?

_____

What items will you need to put inside the kit?

1.	2.	3.	4.	5.
6.	7.	8.	9.	10.

Think about who, what where, when, and why. Do you have an answer for all of your items? Is there anything that you couldn't answer? Practice with a friend, teacher, or caregiver on answering the five Ws for all your items.

you need to know

The first thing you do in the morning will set the pace for the rest of the day. Getting up and ready for the world requires a routine that will ensure you are set for the day. Things like brushing teeth, showering, deodorant, shaving, and making breakfast are a part of almost everyone's day. Using checklists is a great way to help remember what you need to do every morning. This way, you are less likely to forget anything.

Debbie wakes each morning and uses a checklist to make sure she leaves the house with everything. On the kitchen refrigerator she has a whiteboard reminding her what to bring to work. Wallet, phone, house keys, and identification card are all on the list. She checks off each item as she checks her purse. As she goes down the list, she realizes she does not have her house keys. She finds the table where she always leaves her keys and puts them in her purse. Now she is ready to leave the house.

If Debbie had left the house without using the checklist, she may have been locked out of her house upon returning home. Because she used the list, she left the house with everything she needed for the day.

Jesse had a big day ahead. He was going on a job interview at the local supermarket. The night before, he made a checklist of his morning routine. He went through the list. His teeth were brushed, his hair was neat, his clothing was clean, but he had forgotten to shave. Because he checked his list, he then shaved and was ready for the interview. He looked his best, and he got the job.

If Jesse had not used the list, he would not have looked his best. He may still have gotten the job in this case, but to feel and look his best, he made sure to review his checklist so that he had the best chance to get the job.

directions

Use the following tools to help you develop checklists you will need to start your day right. You can download forms for both of these checklists at http://www.newharbinger .com/40644.

What I Need to Start My Day

List all the activities you do upon waking up in the morning to get ready for your day.

1. _____

2. _____

3. _____

4. _____

5. _____

6. _____

7. _____

8. _____

9. _____

10. _____

Think about the order of importance. Which things do you do first? Did you remember everything?

_____

_____

_____

What I Need to Take with Me

List all the things you need when leaving the house for school or work.

1. _____
2. _____
3. _____
4. _____
5. _____
6. _____
7. _____
8. _____
9. _____
10. _____

Choose some items. Thinking about cause and effect, write what would happen if you forgot to bring the item with you.

Item	What would happen if you forgot it?

take note

Use this mirror checklist every morning to make sure your daily routine starts off well. As you read the list, check the box if you can answer yes to any question that applies to you. If not, make sure to take care of that item and add it to your routine. This checklist can also be downloaded at http://www.newharbinger.com/40644.

	Sun	Mon	Tues	Wed	Thurs	Fri	Sat
Are my teeth clean?							
Is my face clean?							
Is my hair brushed?							
Did I use deodorant?							
Is my clothing clean and neat?							
Are my shoes tied and on correctly?							
Did I shave?							
Are my glasses clean?							
Anything else? _____							
Anything else? _____							

you need to know

Good grooming goes beyond your body; it also includes your clothing. Taking care of your clothing and having specific clothing ready for the season is important. A broken zipper on your winter jacket could leave you out in the cold! In addition, certain clothing requires certain types of cleaning; for example, some items don't go in the dryer because they could get ruined.

When going to work, keeping your attire or uniform clean is part of the job. Showing up messy could get you fired. There is a lot to know. Let's take a look at seasonal wear as well as how to care for clothing properly.

The first snow of winter fell. John took out his hat and gloves. He went to the closet where he hung his jackets and took out his winter coat. He put on his winter gear and went out in the snow. After walking a few blocks, John felt something strange. His feet were cold and wet. The sneakers he was wearing did not protect his feet from the snow. He returned home to change into his snow boots. But when he tried to lace them up, he realized that one of his shoelaces was broken. He had forgotten to replace it last winter. Stuck inside, John was unable to go on his errands.

John decided to stay in and do laundry instead. He took his laundry bag and dumped it into the washing machine. He then measured the laundry detergent and put it into the compartment marked for it. He set the water temperature for "warm," as his helper had taught him. About a half hour later, the machine buzzed, signaling that the laundry was complete. He emptied the machine, putting the clothing in a basket and then transferring it to the dryer. He set the timer for forty minutes and went upstairs to make a snack. Forty minutes later, the dryer buzzed and his laundry was complete. All he needed to do was to fold his clothing and put it away.

As he folded his clothing, John felt chilly, so he looked through the pile of clothes for his red sweater. John immediately noticed that the sweater was much smaller than when he had put it in the laundry! How did this happen? The label on the sweater read, "Do not put in dryer," but John had done just that. As a result, the sweater shrank, and John would have to discard his favorite sweater.

There are two lessons for John to take away here. First, at the end of the season, make sure everything is ready for the next season. The day he needed his snow boots came, and he had not checked that his winter gear was ready. Second, read the labels on garments and follow the instructions carefully to avoid ruining your clothing.

directions

Different types of weather and different settings require different types of clothing. Make a list of clothing that you may need specifically for each of these.

Cold, snowy weather

_____

_____

_____

_____

Hot weather

_____

_____

_____

_____

Rainy weather

_____

_____

_____

_____

Beach days

_____

_____

_____

_____

take note

Where do you do your laundry? _____

Many articles of clothing require special care, such as dry cleaning. Where in your community would you find a service that can take care of items that need special care? If you are unsure, how can you find out?

_____

_____

_____

Clothing repairs and cleaning special items costs money. Let's say you bring a shirt to the dry cleaners for cleaning. What is one question you should ask before agreeing to the service?

_____

_____

Some repairs on clothing require special skills, like sewing. Can you sew? If not, how could you learn? Would videos or people you know be able to help?

_____

_____

Where would you take the following items that need repair?

Broken zipper _____

Worn-down heel of a shoe _____

Ripped jeans _____

Tear in a suit jacket _____

Read the labels from each of the clothing items. Briefly explain how you would clean the item.

100% Cotton
Machine wash cold
Do not bleach
Tumble dry
Made from organic cotton

Made in USA
Wash gently in cold water
Do not use high heat
Poly/cotton blend
Made from organic cotton

_____   _____

_____   _____

_____   _____

_____   _____

100% Silk

Dry clean only

Do not use bleach

Colors will run

Wash in cold water

Tumble dry

Do not soak

Made in China

_____

_____

_____

Hand wash or machine wash delicate

Wash with similar colors

Tumble dry low

Stretch-proof fabric

Iron low using protective cloth

95% Cotton, 5% Spandex

Normal process

Non-chlorine bleach only

Prewash for better results

Iron at maximum temperature

---

healthy eating habits

you need to know

What you eat affects your health. It can also affect your mood, stamina, and energy level. Eating habits are important to monitor. For example, if you have a sweet tooth, you cannot give in to every impulse you have for sweets. You must balance your intake of sweets with other healthy choices or you may develop health problems.

Always talk with a doctor when you have questions about your diet or when you are about to make major changes in what you eat. You need to know about any allergies you may have or learn about any foods that you may not be able to eat for other health reasons. A doctor will help you choose the best plan to keep fit and healthy.

What should you eat? Well, that depends on the individual. However, you can use a basic guideline to help choose a balanced diet. These recommendations are based on what the U.S. Department of Health and Human Services outlines for us in maintaining a healthy diet.

What to include in your diet	What you should avoid
Grains (Examples: bread, cereal, oats)	Sugary drinks (Examples: soda and even most fruit juices)
Vegetables (Examples: carrots, peas, broccoli)	Junk food (Examples: processed cakes and cookies, processed snacks like chips)
Fruit (Examples: oranges, apples, peaches, plums, kiwifruit)	Fast food (Most chain restaurant meals are high in salt and calories with little nutritional value.)
Dairy products (Examples: milk, cheese, yogurt)	Any foods with added sugar (High fructose corn syrup is a commonly added sugar.)
Protein foods (Examples: chicken, beef, pork, fish)	Put simply, if a meat product looks like it was made in a factory, then it's probably bad for you. A good rule to remember is that real food doesn't need an ingredients list because real food *is* the ingredient.

Don't forget to do a little more research, and also ask your doctor about how much of each group you should be eating. See the website www.choosemyplate.gov to get more details.

Dallas loves junk food and often fills up on sugary drinks; fast food; and candy, chips, and donuts. His doctor has warned Dallas that if he keeps eating this way, he may develop serious health problem, like obesity, diabetes, and other health-related issues. Dallas usually has problems with his stamina; he is always tired and cannot get work done easily.

Dallas decides he needs to change his eating habits. He follows a new diet based on the recommendations of the Department of Health and Human Services and writes down his food intake daily. By using checklists and reading nutrition books, he makes a big shift from junk food to healthy dietary habits. On his next visit to the doctor, he receives great news. The diet has made his general health much better. In addition to feeling great, Dallas has more energy, and he is doing a much better job at work.

directions

Think about the outline of food groups you just read. List those foods you usually eat that would fit into the group.

The grains I eat are _____

_____

_____

The vegetables I eat are _____

_____

_____

The fruits I eat are _____

_____

_____

The dairy products I eat are _____

_____

_____

The protein foods I eat are _____

_____

_____

Notice that the food groups do not include things like salt, sugar, or fats. A healthy diet includes very small amounts of these items, which are often present in things like candy, chips, or cakes. Make a list of foods you eat that don't easily fit into one of the basic food groups.

What foods in your diet don't fit into the food groups?

_____

_____

What ingredients might be considered unhealthy in these foods?

_____

_____

take note

Use a measuring cup to measure out what a serving might look like. For example, use a one-cup measuring device and measure out one cup of pasta. Is that the amount you might eat for dinner, or would it be more? Look for other foods to measure in your home, and compare a serving to what you would normally eat. For example, while one slice of cheese may equal one serving, how many slices would you put on a sandwich?

Use the chart on the next page to document what you eat in a single day. Put each item you eat in a category. For example, a glass of milk would go in dairy, and a slice of bread would go in grains. If something does not fit into those categories or is on the list of "foods to avoid," put it in the column labeled "Other." What changes might you make after examining your diet for a few days?

Grains	Vegetables	Fruit	Dairy	Protein foods	Other

15 navigating the community

you need to know

Going out and about may be part of your daily routine. Some people travel independently, and others travel with another adult. Either way, you must have the proper skills to keep yourself safe. There is a lot to pay attention to when you are out in the community. Crossing a busy street requires careful attention to the traffic signs, the flow of cars, and any obstructions in the road. Being safe is the primary goal. Traffic, pedestrians, and bike riders are all around you. You must be aware of them all to keep yourself from getting injured.

If you are using public transportation, you also have a lot to think about. For example, just knowing the routes of buses and trains can be overwhelming. You always need to check the routes of the train or bus you are using so you don't get lost. Along the way, make sure you are aware of the stop you're at. In addition, make sure you plan your trips correctly to ensure you arrive on time.

Todd is going to the grocery store. It is about a ten-minute walk from his house. He leaves his building and turns down a street, making sure to walk on the sidewalk and not in the street. He arrives at the corner and has to cross a busy street. He looks at the traffic light. The Don't Walk sign is flashing, so he waits. He also looks both ways to get a sense of traffic. The sign then changes to Walk. Before he crosses, he looks both ways again even though the sign says Walk, because there is always the chance that a car could go through the red light. He crosses the street briskly, not running, but not too slow. As he crosses, he keeps his eyes on the traffic. He then steps up on the curb and successfully gets across the street.

Josh gets on the bus and is heading to Fifty-Ninth Street. He pays the fare. He then takes the first open seat. The bus stops at every other street only on even numbered blocks. As he rides the bus, he checks the street number to make sure he doesn't miss his stop. He uses the park as a landmark to remind him that he will be getting off at the next stop. The bus passes the park and Todd rings the bell, signaling he would like to get off. When the bus stops at Sixtieth Street, he gets off and walks back one block to his destination.

Both travelers did all the right things to keep themselves safe and on track to get to their destinations. There were a lot of steps each person took to get to where he was going. Let's do a few activities to help us recognize these steps.

directions

Circle True or False for each statement. Explain why you answered the way you did.

1. You may cross in the middle of the street if no cars are coming.　　True　　False

    _____

    _____

2. You need to look only in the direction of traffic when crossing the street.　　True　　False

    _____

    _____

3. It is okay to wear headphones when crossing the street.　　True　　False

    _____

    _____

4. If no traffic is coming, you can cross when the sign says   True   False
   Don't Walk.

   _____

   _____

5. If you have the right of way, you don't have to worry about cars   True   False
   turning when you cross.

   _____

   _____

6. Landmarks won't help you know which direction you are going.   True   False

   _____

   _____

7. When you are riding a bus, the driver always lets you know when   True   False
   it is your stop.

   _____

   _____

8. If no one is sitting next to you on the bus, it is okay to put your   True   False
   feet up if you are tired.

   _____

   _____

(All answers were false. These were all examples of bad habits when traveling and things that can put you in danger. Review each situation and think about what might happen if someone uses bad habits.)

take note

You are about to cross a busy street. What steps will you need to take before you cross?

_____

_____

_____

When riding public transportation, what are some things to keep in mind?

_____

_____

_____

Using landmarks is important to getting around town. What landmarks do you use to help you differentiate between north, south, east, and west? Find landmarks in your community to help you find directions.

_____

_____

_____

Think about a place you travel to frequently. How would you get there on your own? What steps do you need to take to get to your destination?

_____

_____

_____

You are walking to a destination and realize you are lost. You look around but don't recognize any landmarks. What would you do?

_____

_____

_____

you need to know

Keeping a safe home requires an understanding of basic maintenance and potential hazards. Fires and other emergencies can happen in the home if you don't monitor your environment. Simple actions like making sure the stove is turned off or unplugging appliances can prevent serious or dangerous situations. You probably cannot take care of everything by yourself. If something seems unsafe, like an electrical outlet or a light switch, you may have to call an electrician, the landlord, or the superintendent of your home. If your refrigerator stops working, who would you call? If it took some time to get it fixed, should you eat any of the food in the refrigerator? Definitely not. There are many things we need to look at around our home to keep it safe.

Donald was cooking a meal at the stove when the telephone rang. As he ran to pick it up, he knocked into a pan handle that had been sticking out from the stove. The pan fell off the stove, spilling hot oil. Fortunately, Donald was not hurt. He did learn a valuable lesson: to make sure pot handles and pan handles were turned in, not sticking out from the stove.

* * *

Rita was charging her iPhone and iPad in the living room. She also wanted to plug in her radio and the vacuum cleaner. The power strip was full, so she plugged another power strip into the first one. When she turned on the vacuum, the power went out. She learned that you cannot plug too many items into one socket.

* * *

Frank was making tea. He put the water on the stove and then went into the living room to read. After a while, he decided to go to bed, forgetting about the water on the stove. In a few hours, the water evaporated and the kettle began to smoke. He awoke to a house filled with smoke and a ruined teakettle. Fortunately, no one was hurt. He learned that he needed to make sure to check the stove every night before going to bed.

All three of these examples could have been avoided if safety checks and protocols were put in place. It is important to always be ready for an emergency as well as do everything you can to prevent one.

directions

What safety lessons are learned in each of these scenarios?

Rachel has not checked the batteries in the smoke alarm for over a year. One night there was a small electrical fire. Fortunately, she smelled the smoke and put out the fire, but the alarm never went off.

Lesson learned? _____

_____

_____

Artie opened the refrigerator, and it didn't feel cold. He poured a glass of milk. He forgot about the refrigerator and made dinner. Later, he was very sick because the food had spoiled. When his caregiver came for a visit, she called a refrigerator repairman and the refrigerator was fixed.

Lesson learned? _____

_____

_____

Tess woke up in the morning and found that someone had entered her apartment in the middle of the night and taken money and jewelry. She called the police, who found that she had left her door unlocked the night before.

Lesson learned? _____

_____

_____

Jodi was making toast and went to plug in the toaster. The toaster was old, and the wires were worn. When she plugged it in, she received a painful electric shock. Her sister came over later and wrapped the wire in electrical tape.

Lesson learned? _____

_____

_____

take note

Go through your home with this checklist. Make sure all items on the list are checked off. This will help make your home safe.

Checklist for the Home

☐ Emergency telephone numbers are kept on a list near the phone.

☐ All your smoke and carbon monoxide detectors have been checked and are in working order.

☐ Halls and stairs are free of clutter.

☐ Electrical cords are kept safely out of the way.

☐ Tall bookcases and stands are secured to the wall to prevent them from tipping over.

☐ High shelves are safely accessible with a secure stepstool.

☐ Window guards are placed in the windows if children live in the home.

☐ Windows and doors are easy to open.

☐ Locks are easy to operate.

☐ A night-light is available to provide light when needed.

☐ Stairs and steps are well lit.

☐ Any firearms in the home are kept properly locked away.

☐ You have a clear escape plan in case of emergency.

Kitchen

☐ Pot handles are turned inward on the stove.

☐ Glass objects and sharp blades are put away correctly.

☐ The stove is clean inside and out.

☐ A kitchen fire extinguisher is kept near the stove.

☐ Curtains, rags, and other flammable items are not placed near the stove.

☐ Pot holders and oven mitts are easily available.

Bathroom

☐ Floors are covered with nonslip pads.

☐ The tub or shower has a bar or handle for easy access or to hold for stability.

☐ A bath or shower seat is available if needed.

☐ Medications are stored securely in medicine cabinet.

☐ Electrical appliances are not located near the sink, tub, or shower.

Home Escape Plan

☐ Have several paths out of each room.

☐ Know how to crawl low to the floor when escaping toxic smoke.

☐ Know that you should not return to the home during emergency.

☐ Have an established meeting point after the escape.

☐ Practice the escape plan.

Smoking

☐ Anyone who smokes uses fire-safe cigarettes.

☐ Smoking takes place only outside the home.

☐ Matches and lighters are stored securely.

☐ Ashtrays are large and deep and kept away from anything that can catch fire.

☐ Ashtrays are emptied into a container that cannot burn, such as a fire bucket or metal can.

take note

To ensure the safety of your home, review this checklist nightly before going to bed. At http://www.newharbinger.com/40644 you can download a copy of this checklist.

Nightly Checklist

☐ Doors are locked and secure.

☐ Any appliance that does not need to be plugged in is unplugged.

☐ The stovetop and oven are turned off.

☐ The washing machine and dryer are not running.

☐ Candles or cigarettes are extinguished properly.

☐ Exits are neat and clear.

☐ Gas and electric heaters are turned off or safely placed in the room.

☐ Internal doors are kept closed in case of fire.

in case of emergency 17

you need to know

In case of emergency, dial 911. Make that call any time there is a situation of life or death. It is simple. Even when your smartphone is locked you can make an emergency call. There is usually a place on the locked smartphone screen that says Emergency. You must make this call only in the case of a real emergency. If you have a problem that is not serious, 911 is not the number to call. Let's take a look at a few scenarios to decide what an emergency is and what it isn't.

John smells smoke. He looks out the window and sees smoke coming out from a neighbor's house. The smoke is black and getting thicker. He immediately calls 911 and says, "There is smoke coming from my neighbor's house." The woman at the other end asks for the address and tells John a fire truck is on the way. In a few minutes, the fire truck arrives and puts out a small fire in the neighbor's kitchen. The firemen tell John it was a good thing he called because the fire could have gotten much worse.

Francesca smells gas in her apartment. She checks her stove; it is turned off. She looks around for where the smell is coming from. Finding nothing, she dials 911 and tells the operator she smells gas in her apartment but doesn't know where it is coming from. The operator tells her that help is on the way. In a few minutes, the fire department and the gas company send help. They find a gas leak coming from the basement of the apartment building. It could have been a serious problem if Francesca had not called 911.

Willa is in the park and sees a man fall down. He is unconscious and not moving. She immediately calls 911 and explains the situation. An ambulance comes quickly and gives the man treatment. He is okay. They put him on a stretcher and take him to the nearest hospital. The emergency medical service person tells Willa it was a good thing she called; she saved the man's life.

In all these situations it was important to dial 911. These situations could have resulted in serious injury or even death if the person did not call for help. Remember, 911 is always the number to call when there is an emergency.

directions

Each of these scenarios may or may not be an emergency. Circle Yes if you think the situation is serious enough to call 911. Circle No if you think a call to 911 is not indicated.

You have lost your keys. Dial 911?   Yes or No

You witness a car accident. Dial 911?   Yes or No

Someone is mean to you at the store. Dial 911?   Yes or No

You see someone lying on the street, bleeding. Dial 911?   Yes or No

You take the wrong bus. Dial 911?   Yes or No

You have a stomachache. Dial 911?   Yes or No

You fall and cannot get up. Dial 911?   Yes or No

Your caregiver or parent won't let you do something you want to do. Dial 911?   Yes or No

The next questions require you to call 911. What would you say to the operator in these situations?

1. You smell smoke but don't see anything. The smell gets stronger and stronger.

    _____

    _____

    _____

    _____

2. You see a man on the street leaning against the wall, clutching his chest. You ask if he is okay but he does not respond.

    _____

    _____

    _____

    _____

take note

If you are not feeling well, you may want to call a doctor. Feeling sick may require a doctor's appointment. Write down the name and address of the doctor you would use. Include the telephone number.

Doctor's name _____

Address _____

Phone number _____

If you see a leaky fire hydrant or have a question about fire safety, you don't need to call 911. You might want to call your local fire station. Keep this information for your local fire department handy.

Firehouse precinct or station number _____

Address _____

Phone number _____

If you have a question for the police department, you may want to call your local police station directly. Nonemergency issues should be addressed at the local police station. Fill in the information about your local police station.

Police precinct _____

Address _____

Phone number _____

If you use any other local agencies or services, write down the information here.

Agency _____

Address _____

Phone number _____

Agency _____

Address _____

Phone number _____

Agency _____

Address _____

Phone number _____

Agency _____

Address _____

Phone number _____

Agency _____

Address _____

Phone number _____

18 public vs. private information

you need to know

Private information includes your Social Security number, credit card numbers, telephone number, and address, to name a few. Any numbers like bank account information and passwords are also personal information. You must be very careful how you share this information. This information can be stolen and used by someone else to make purchases or hack into accounts. Giving out private information over the phone or in an email can lead to serious problems. Identity theft is when someone gets hold of your private information and uses it for his or her own benefit. It happens quite frequently.

Let's take a look at some ways to keep your private information safe.

Sid gets a phone call from a woman claiming to be from the Social Security office. She says there is a problem with his taxes and he needs to provide his Social Security number. Sid knows never to give personal or private information over the phone when someone calls. He tells her to give him her phone number and he will call back to verify the office. The caller hangs up. Sid did the right thing. This is a type of scamming. A caller calls and claims to need personal information. The caller can make it sound serious. However, Sid knows that no government agency asks for private information over the phone.

* * *

Warren receives an email from a bank claiming there is a problem with his account. They ask that he immediately send his Social Security number, bank account number, and any passwords needed to enter his online account. Warren knows that he should never give this information over email. He goes to the bank and tells them what happened. The bank manager says the bank never asks for this information over email and he should report the email to the authorities.

✱ ✱ ✱

Lydia receives a phone call from someone who says he is from the telephone company. He states there is a problem with the account and the company needs her credit card information to keep the phone in service. She gives them the credit card number and information. A few weeks later, charges show up on her card that she did not make. Her credit card has been used fraudulently. She calls the company and tells them what happened. The credit card company tells her never to give this information over the phone when someone calls.

directions

Decide whether each scenario is safe or unsafe to share private information. Circle the correct answer.

1.	Putting your Social Security number on a job application	safe	unsafe
2.	Putting your phone number on social media	safe	unsafe
3.	Giving your bank password to a friend	safe	unsafe
4.	Using a credit card in a store	safe	unsafe
5.	Sharing any private information on a call you receive	safe	unsafe
6.	Writing your Social Security number on a tax form	safe	unsafe
7.	Sending an email with your credit card number	safe	unsafe
8.	Entering a credit card number on a website like Amazon or eBay	safe	unsafe
9.	Putting your address on Facebook	safe	unsafe
10.	Lending your friend a credit card	safe	unsafe

Answers: Scenarios 1, 4, 6, and 8 are safe. Scenarios 2, 3, 5, 7, 9, and 10 are unsafe.

Let's take a look at the situations that are unsafe in these questions. Can you give advice to a friend who is in each of these situations?

A friend wants to put his number on Facebook. Tell him why this is a bad idea.

_____

_____

_____

A friend asks what your bank password is. Why shouldn't you tell her?

_____

_____

_____

Your friend gets a phone call asking for private information including his Social Security number. He asks you what he should do. What do you tell him?

_____

_____

_____

Your sister gets an email asking for her phone number and address. It also asks for her bank account information. What do you tell her?

_____

_____

_____

You notice a friend has put her address on Facebook. You tell her it is not good to share private information on social media. Explain why.

_____

_____

_____

A friend wants to borrow your credit card and says he will pay you back. What do you tell him?

_____

_____

_____

take note

Explain what private information is. Tell why it should be kept private.

_____

_____

_____

Make a list of things that contain private information and things you should never share.

_____

_____

_____

Keeping private information safe includes keeping the information in a safe place. Where do you keep information that is private?

_____

_____

_____

When you are unsure about sharing information, or if you are unsure if information is private, who can you speak with?

_____

_____

_____

you need to know

Keeping good records helps you find and share information you may need to share, perhaps with medical, educational, or financial experts. Having good records can protect you from any issues regarding your finances or personal health. For example, keeping receipts organized will help you do your taxes; if any issues arise, the receipts may be used as proof that your taxes were done correctly. On another note, checking your credit card receipts every month will alert you if anyone has made a purchase without your authorization. If you keep these records organized, they are easily retrievable so you can show the credit card company the problem.

Here are three good habits to develop:

- Save receipts. You should save any receipts that affect your taxes for three years. This doesn't mean you have to save the receipt from your morning coffee purchase. Save those receipts you are going to use for tax purposes. Save credit card statements for three years as well.

- Create a space at home where you can keep documents and work on them when necessary.

- Use an online bookkeeping program to manage your finances and appointments.

Jared moved to a new state. After settling in, he found a new doctor and made an appointment. Because Jared was a new patient, the doctor asked him about his health history. Jared kept good records and brought all his medical documents from past doctors' appointments, including checkup information and medications he needed. After reading all Jared's records, the doctor was able to provide him with the appropriate medical care. Jared also needed to open a new bank account. He went to the bank with all his financial documents, including his old bank account number. The bank easily opened a new account for him.

When Sally got her credit card bill, it seemed very high. She looked over the bill and did not see any obvious errors. She called the company and said the bill seemed high. The company told her to review past bills and see if there were any unauthorized charges. She said she did not have them. The company sent the last six months of bills to her, and she reviewed them. It turned out that three months ago she had been charged for a television set she did not purchase. If she had kept the records, she would have saved a lot of time and effort.

In these examples we see how good record keeping makes life easy, and poor record keeping leads to big problems. Keeping good records keeps your money and important documents safe and helps protect your health and finances.

directions

Take a look at the documents and receipts you keep. Use these categories to list what documents you have or need. Make sure the right documents go into the right categories.

Receipts: **List the type of receipts you should keep**

_____

_____

_____

_____

_____

_____

_____

_____

_____

Financial Documents

_____

_____

_____

_____

_____

_____

_____

_____

_____

_____

_____

Medical Documents

_____

_____

_____

_____

_____

_____

_____

_____

_____

_____

Education Records

_____

_____

_____

_____

_____

_____

_____

_____

_____

Miscellaneous Records

_____

_____

_____

_____

_____

_____

_____

_____

_____

You can download blank copies of these lists at http://www.newharbinger.com/40644.

take note

What system do you have for storing and maintaining your records? Folders? Envelopes?

_____

_____

_____

_____

Describe the benefits of keeping good records.

_____

_____

_____

_____

What other categories of record keeping might be helpful to you?

_____

_____

_____

_____

Do you use an online bookkeeping system? How could using a system like this help you?

_____

_____

_____

_____

Different financial records should be held for certain amounts of time. Take a look at http://IRS.gov, and see if you can list how long you should keep financial records.

20 who can help?

you need to know

You should now know what to do in the case of an emergency (see activity 17), but there are times that you may need help when it is not an emergency. Asking the right people the right questions is important and can help you get things done successfully. Sometimes the help you need can be found with a simple phone call or Internet search. It is easier than ever to get information when you need help.

James is in his kitchen making a snack. He notices that there is a puddle of water under his refrigerator. He looks underneath and sees that the refrigerator is leaking. James lives in an apartment building. He isn't sure what to do. James calls his mother. His mother says, "Next to the phone is the number of the building handyman. Call him and tell him what the problem is." James calls the building handyman and explains that his refrigerator is leaking. The handyman comes right away and makes the repairs.

James could have called the handyman himself, but he needed a little reminder. It was smart to call his mother, who gave him good advice. It is good to have someone to rely on when you need help with a situation that is not an emergency.

Wanda comes home from her day program and is ready to watch some television. When she presses the power button, the television won't turn on. She then realizes that the lights also won't go on. It seems that the power in her house is off. She is not sure what to do and decides to go to bed early. When she gets home the next night, the same thing happens. She has no power for a week. Finally, her sister comes to visit. Her sister tells her that when the power goes out she needs to call someone—in this case, the power company. They look at Wanda's electric bill and find the phone number. Someone from the company comes out and fixes the problem. Wanda now has power.

Wanda should have never waited so long to ask for help or call the power company. If you have a problem, get help right away.

directions

Work with a teacher or caregiver to decide which professional would be best to call to get help.

You pick up a prescription from the pharmacy. When you get home, you realize you don't know how much medication to take. Your doctor is out of town. Who can you call?

_____

You need to find a new dentist. You have a good insurance plan, but you don't know any dentists in town. Who can help you?

_____

You are having problems with your front-door lock and cannot get into your apartment. Your lock seems to be broken. Who can work on the lock?

_____

Your smartphone is not taking a charge. Where can you get help? Who can you call?

_____

You are at work and find that the scanner you use is not working. Who would you go to to help solve the problem?

_____

Your oven isn't working, and you can't cook dinner. Who are you going to call?

_____

take note

When you have a problem that you cannot solve on your own, who is your go-to person or people? List them here.

_____

_____

_____

Make a list of service providers or professionals you have called in the past to fix problems.

_____ to help with _____

_____ to help with _____

_____ to help with _____

_____ to help with _____

_____ to help with _____

_____ to help with _____

Take a look around the house. Are there any problems that might come up where you will need to call a professional? Do a little research and find some providers that you can call.

Call _____ if _____

Call _____ if _____

Call _____ if _____

Call _____ if _____

Call _____ if _____

Part 3

Leisure Time

Leisure time is essential to your health. It helps improve your overall well-being and attitude, and it is good for your social life. It can also help your physical fitness. It keeps your mind active and provides the tools for keeping you in a good mood.

Boredom is not a good feeling. People don't spend their time just working; they find hobbies, activities with friends, and other interests to fill their free time in order to keep busy and strengthen their quality of life. Finding something to do in your downtime takes some planning. The activities in this part will help you think about what things are of interest and how you can develop them in your free time. It is good to have more than one interest. If you like soccer, you may not be able to play in the winter, so having options will be important year-round.

Your own leisure time can be expanded and explored with a few simple tools. First, it is important to think about what activities you have an interest in. Exploring those interests may lead you to a whole world related to that interest that you may not have thought about. Perhaps you like video games. Video games are great, but there may be more to gaming than you thought. You might like to take a coding class to create your own video games. There are lots of books to read about video games as well. There are social groups dedicated to sharing information about video games. So instead of sitting alone and playing, there are many options for those who like to play video games.

Let's take a look at some activities that will help you start thinking about your free time. Think about what you like to do on your own and with other people. You should always be in charge of your leisure time. You should speak up about how you want to spend your time off from school and work.

21 interest inventory

you need to know

Making a list of interests can help you organize things you like to do, as well as help expand that interest. You should also think about what is realistic. Perhaps you like airplanes. Flying an airplane is not something everyone can do. However, you can read books, build models, and even take a flight. An interest needs to work for you. To participate fully in your leisure time, the interest should be accessible, realistic for your circumstances, and within your budget.

Felicia loves to draw. She spends all her free time drawing. Her day program gives her plenty of time to draw, but Felicia wants to broaden this interest into other areas that will encourage her to socialize and expand her talents. Felicia meets with her counselor to talk about options. Her counselor tells her about an art class she can participate in at a local school. The counselor also tells her about weekly museum trips where she can see a variety of artwork.

After a few weeks, Felicia participates in the art class and goes on her first museum trip. Felicia loves both new activities. She makes new friends and shares her artwork with them. Felicia's artwork is better than ever. She has also taken up painting and sculpture as a result of learning about these new media from her museum trips.

directions

Answer these questions about your interests and favorite things.

What are your hobbies (or things you like to do for fun)?

_____

_____

_____

If you take any lessons or classes that support your interests, write about them here.

_____

_____

_____

What kind of activities do you do by yourself?

_____

_____

_____

What kind of activities do you do with friends?

_____

_____

_____

When at home, what do you spend most of your time doing?

_____

_____

_____

Write down any leisure activities you'd like to explore.

_____

_____

_____

Check the subjects you like or liked to do most in school.

Art _____   Math _____   Reading _____   Writing _____   Science _____

Physical education _____   Music _____   Social studies _____

Other _____

Of the subjects you checked, are there any hobbies or interests related to those subjects?

_____

_____

_____

take note

When looking over the answers to your questions, are there any topics or themes that stand out for you?

_____

_____

_____

What are your top three favorite activities?

_____

_____

_____

How often are you able to engage in your favorite activities?

_____

_____

_____

Where can you go to get more information about your interests?

_____

_____

_____

Do you feel you have enough time to engage in your favorite activities? How much time would you like?

_____

_____

_____

Think about one activity. If you were to expand this interest, how could you do this? Who could help you?

_____

_____

_____

the differences between work and hobbies 22

you need to know

Thinking about a career path is not the same as engaging in a hobby. There are going to be differences in most cases. A hobby may not lead to a career. You may be interested in singing. However, following a career path as a singer is difficult and requires a certain amount of talent. You may want to work with animals. This doesn't automatically mean you can become a veterinarian, which takes years of schooling and intense training.

This is not to say you cannot find work in a field that interests you. In fact, it is something to be encouraged. But your leisure time is more about relaxation and spending quality time on your own and with friends.

Beth is interested in animals and looks for work as a veterinarian. Unfortunately, her learning disability has made it difficult to earn college credits. After meeting with her counselor, she is directed to an animal shelter where she is able to volunteer her time caring for cats and dogs. This is the perfect way to spend some of her free time, as she loves taking care of the animals. Becoming a veterinarian is unrealistic for Beth because she cannot complete the advance coursework needed to get the degree. However, she has found a way to pursue her love of animals.

Wendy wants to be a professional basketball player, but she has never been on a team, nor has she ever been coached. She works with her caregiver to find a local basketball clinic where she can play on a local team with a coach. After participating in a few sessions, she finds she loves it and enjoys spending a few hours a week on the team. Becoming a professional basketball player requires a lifetime of practice and dedication. In addition, not every great player is chosen to play professionally. But that did not stop Wendy from making basketball a hobby she now regularly engages in.

directions

Some careers require an advanced degree or a specific skill or talent that is not available to all people. However, there may be related activities that can often lead to a hobby or a way to spend your leisure time. The left column shows some career paths. What hobbies, leisure activities, or volunteer opportunities can you think of that relate to that field?

Career path	Related hobbies, leisure activities, or volunteer opportunities
Animals	
Sports	
Teaching	
Medical field	
Music	
Construction	
Transportation	

Film/TV	
Art	
Other	

take note

How are careers and hobbies different?

_____

_____

_____

How can you find a hobby related to a career interest that may be out of reach?

_____

_____

_____

If you are working now, does the position you hold relate to any interests or hobbies? If it does, tell what the connection is.

_____

_____

_____

If you have an important hobby or interest, how can that relate to your finding a career?

_____

_____

_____

How can you balance the time you spend at work with your hobby?

_____

_____

_____

finding resources to support your hobbies 23

you need to know

There are lots of ways to support your hobby or leisure time. Finding resources to support your interests can be fun and easy. For example, going to the public library is an easy way to find books and materials about a wide range of topics. You can also use the Internet to find out about almost anything. When you use the Internet, the most important rule of thumb is to make sure you use key words that will specifically help you find information. Let's say you want to use the Internet to find out when and where a certain movie is playing. If you type in only the name of the movie you will get lots of results, but nothing about where the movie would be playing in your area.

Peter is interested in robotics. He loves to build and code in his free time. He goes online to look up some information about robotics coding so he can further develop his programming skills. When he asks the librarian for the section on robotics, he is led to the science fiction section, not the hobby section. After going through the shelves, he does not find anything on robotics coding and programming. He goes back to the librarian and asks for robotics coding and programming books. The librarian then leads him to the right section where he finds the books he needs. Had he given the librarian some more specific information, he would have found the right section at first.

When Peter gets home, he goes on the Internet. He types in "robotics." Thousands of websites pop up. He adds the words "coding and programming," and he types in the city he lives in. He then gets information about local stores that sell kits, sites that offer coding programs, and even local clubs that get together to build robots. This is a lot of information, so he goes through each topic carefully and makes a plan to visit a few stores and to get in touch with the local club.

Being specific when searching for information is key. The more specific you are, the more relevant information you will get.

directions

Develop some key terms relating to your interest or hobby that you would use as a search term for the Internet.

1. My interest _____

   My search terms _____

   _____

2. My interest _____

   My search terms _____

   _____

3. My interest _____

   My search terms _____

   _____

Besides the Internet, where or who could you go to for more information about your interests?

_____

_____

take note

Let's use the Internet to find some information about your interest. After you have finished your search, answer the questions.

What interest did you type in? _____

Was the information specific or relevant to your interest?

_____

What could you add to get better and more specific results?

_____

What about finding information about a movie, play, or special event?

Pick a movie, play, or event you are interested in attending.

_____

Besides the Internet, where could you get information about this movie, play, or event?

_____

What specific information about going to this event do you need?

_____

If you were going to do an Internet search for this activity, what words would you use?

_____

24 sharing your interests

you need to know

Sharing interests and doing things with friends are always fun. It is always a good idea to find friends who share your interests rather than engaging in solitary activities. Going to a movie, going ice skating, or even just taking a trip to the library is something you can share with someone. You have to reach out to friends and find out what their interests are. That way, you can share good times with others. Others can also offer you new opportunities. By including others in your plans, you are more likely to have them include you in their plans.

Brett went to the movies. After the show he met his friend Roger in the lobby. They had both attended the same show. Roger said, "I didn't know you were coming. Next time, let's meet before the show and go together. It will be more fun." Brett agreed. The next week, Brett wants to see a new movie. He calls Roger, who agrees to meet him at the theater. They go together and have a great time.

* * *

Carol and Jennifer both love to paint. Carol finds a painting class at the local community college and wants to go, but she is nervous about going alone. She calls Jennifer and tells her about the class. Jennifer is excited and agrees to sign up. They both attend the class and have a great time. In fact, they meet people who become their friends. Going together made it much easier to try something new.

directions

1. Make a list of your friends and their interests.

Name of friend	Interests

2. Write down the names of any friends who share a common interest with you.

_____

_____

3. How can you share your interests with a friend?

_____

_____

take note

Make a plan to share leisure time or an interest with a friend.

How will you let the friend know you want to share this interest?

_____

_____

_____

Sharing leisure time requires people to be flexible. Your friends may have other interests or ideas of how to spend leisure time. How can you be flexible about including other people's interests in your leisure activities? For example, if someone suggested an activity you have never tried before, you could agree to try it.

_____

_____

_____

Time alone is okay, as long as you balance that time with social activities. What activities do you prefer to do on your own?

_____

_____

Think about a time when you wished to spend time with friends but didn't. What stopped you from inviting someone to join you? What might you do different next time?

_____

_____

_____

_____

25 group activities

you need to know

Participating in a leisure activity with a group requires flexibility and patience. With a group, there are lots of interests and lots of ideas. It means you may have to get involved in something that someone else wants to do. It is an excellent way to try new things and expand your interests. You need to listen and be open to trying something different. You never know when you will find something new and interesting!

Dennis was with his habilitation group, and they were making plans for the day. Most of the group wanted to go to the museum, but Dennis did not want to go. In fact, he refused. He just was not interested. Dennis was being stubborn and would not move from his seat. The rest of the group was angry about Dennis's inflexibility and tried to get him to go. Dennis still refused. The group went without him.

When the group returned, they shared their experience with Dennis. They told him how much fun they had. Dennis did not have fun. He sat by himself all day. He wished he had gone after hearing about the great time everyone had.

The next day, the group wanted to go to see a show. Again, Dennis did not want to go. He remembered how much the group had enjoyed the museum visit, so he decided to join his group even though he really did not want to. At the end of the day, Dennis had a great time. He really enjoyed the show and was glad he had been flexible.

directions

Answer the questions below, thinking about how you could be flexible in the situation.
Some ways to be flexible include:

- Trying hard to accept changes in plans

- Staying calm when things are not what you expect

- Letting other people have their way

- Balancing your interests with those of others

Your friends want to see a movie you don't want to see. All of them agree they want to
go. How do you handle the situation?

_____

_____

_____

_____

Two of your friends want to go to a dance. Another two friends want to go to a museum.
How could you handle this situation? What advice could you give your friends?

_____

_____

_____

_____

You invite a few friends over to watch a program on television. When they get to your house, they decide that they want to watch something different. What is your reaction?

_____

_____

_____

_____

take note

Think about a time that you wanted to do something different than the group. How did you handle it?

_____

_____

_____

_____

Could there have been a better way to handle the situation? If so, what was it?

_____

_____

_____

_____

Think about a time you tried something new or decided to follow your friend's interest. How was that experience for you? Did you learn something new or find a new interest?

_____

_____

_____

_____

Have you ever shared an interest with a friend who enjoyed the experience and maybe even explored it further? How was that experience? How did it make you feel?

_____

_____

_____

_____

26 balancing your time

you need to know

Keeping a balance between work and leisure is important. How much time do you spend at work? How much time do you spend doing leisure activities? The leisure activities you spend time engaged in can vary. Balancing between work and leisure is important, but so is making sure you balance your leisure time. For instance, if you like watching television in your leisure time, you may not be making adequate room for exercise or physical activity. It is important to balance sitting and watching television with activities that improve your health.

Stella watches a lot of television and does not usually leave the house. During a visit to the doctor, the doctor recommends that Stella get some exercise. The doctor says that Stella needs to improve her physical fitness by finding an activity that will help promote good health. Stella loves to swim, so she decides to go to the pool. As a result, she swims every day for a bit and does some exercise on the gym equipment. Because she goes to the gym, she watches less television. She notices that she feels better, is in a better mood, and has a lot more energy than usual. She now has energy to go out with friends once a week. By balancing her life with physical and social activity, she has greatly enhanced her well-being.

directions

Use this chart to document your weekly routines. You can download a blank form at http://www.newharbinger.com/40644. In a word or two, list the activities you do during that time, including leisure activities and work or study. After the week is over, add up the amount of time you spent doing leisure activities and work or study. Compare the two.

Are you getting enough time to engage in leisure?

	Sun	Mon	Tue	Wed	Thurs	Fri	Sat
8:00 a.m.							
9:00 a.m.							
10:00 a.m.							
11:00 a.m.							
12:00 p.m.							
1:00 p.m.							

2:00 p.m.						
3:00 p.m.						
4:00 p.m.						
5:00 p.m.						
6:00 p.m.						
7:00 p.m.						
8:00 p.m.						
9:00 p.m.						
10:00 p.m.						

Total hours spent in leisure activity _____

Total hours spent in work or study _____

take note

What did you learn from documenting your activities for the week?

_____

_____

Do you balance your work and leisure time well? Why or why not?

_____

_____

Are the types of activities balanced between physical and sedentary? How so?

_____

_____

Are the leisure activities balanced between group and solitary activities? How so?

_____

_____

What types of changes could you make to your schedule for better balance?

_____

_____

27 using schedules

you need to know

A schedule is important when managing your time, finding a movie, and checking when the bus comes, and for lots of other things. Schedules will help you avoid missing appointments or having time conflicts. A schedule can be as easy as keeping a list of activities and the times and dates they occur. Most smartphones now have a calendar app that will help you manage your time. In some cities you can text a message and receive a bus schedule. Keeping a schedule and using schedules will help you get where you are going on time.

Troy uses schedules all day. When he wakes up, he checks his smartphone and sees that he has a doctor's appointment at 1:00. He is going to go by bus and checks the schedule of bus departures. He finds the correct bus; it is leaving at 12:30, which will give him plenty of time to get to the appointment.

Later that night, he is going to a movie. He looks up the theater and finds the movie he wants to see. He uses the movie timetable to find the times that the movie is playing. He gets to the movie using the bus. He checks the schedule again and finds a bus that will take him there and home afterward. When Troy gets home, he looks at his calendar and sees that tomorrow he has an interview at 2:00 and is meeting friends for dinner at 6:00.

The next day Troy goes to all his appointments. His friends want to get together on Friday, so he marks it down in his calendar. By using schedules, Troy has a productive and fun week.

directions

Use the schedules to help plan your activities for the week.

1. Use this bus schedule to plan your trip.

M15 Bus Schedule	
To Central City	To Johnsville
11:00 a.m.	11:15 a.m.
12:05 p.m.	12:20 p.m.
1:13 p.m.	1:48 p.m.
2:20 p.m.	2:44 p.m.
3:35 p.m.	3:55 p.m.
4:40 p.m.	5:30 p.m.
5:10 p.m.	6:15 p.m.
6:12 p.m.	7:17 p.m.
7:33 p.m.	7:50 p.m.

You are taking the bus to Central City for a 2:00 p.m. movie. The bus takes thirty minutes to get to Central City. Which bus will you take to get to the movie on time?

_____

The movie is two hours long. You will take the bus back to Johnsville when the movie is over. Which bus can you take?

_____

You are going to meet friends for dinner at 5:00 p.m. in Central City. The restaurant is a five-minute walk from the bus station. Dinner will last about two hours. Which bus do you take to Central City? Which bus can you take home to Johnsville?

_____

2. Use the schedule to help manage your week. Put the events in the calendar.

Sun, May 1	Mon, May 2	Tues, May 3	Weds, May 4	Thurs, May 5	Fri, May 6	Sat, May 7

Add the following:

- May 4, basketball practice at 1:00 p.m.

- Thursday, dinner with friends at 6:00 p.m.

- Tuesday, doctor's appointment at 11:00 a.m.

- Saturday, movies with friends at 1:00 p.m.

- May 1, call Mom for her birthday

- May 2, work from 8:00 a.m. to 3:00 p.m.

- May 5, work from 8:00 a.m. to 3:00 p.m.

- Sunday, art class 9:00 a.m. to 11:00 a.m.

- May 3, meeting with supervisor at 3:00 p.m.

- May 4, meet friends for lunch at 1:00 p.m.

After filling in your schedule, did you notice any conflicts? If so, what were they?

_____

Is there a way you can fix the conflict? What would make sense to change?

_____

Another friend calls and asks you to go to a museum. What day and time could you go, based on your schedule?

_____

take note

In your daily life, how and when do you use schedules?

_____

_____

_____

How do you keep track of your appointments? Do you use pen and paper? Digital?

_____

_____

_____

How do you plan your day to ensure that you can make it to your appointments on time?

_____

_____

_____

Think about a time you had trouble being on time or keeping an appointment. What circumstances would have helped you to get there on time or make the appointment?

_____

_____

_____

budgeting for leisure 28

you need to know

Some leisure activities and hobbies require money. There are also plenty of things to fill your leisure time that don't cost money. Having a balance between the two is helpful for keeping you within your leisure budget. You can't always do the things you want if you don't have the money. There are also ways of saving money, like seeing an early movie at a discount or finding museum days that might be free. The bottom line is that you must know how much you can spend before you engage in any activity or make any purchases.

Roger enjoys video games. He goes on line almost every day and orders a new game. By the end of the week, he has gone through all of his disposable income, and his game collection is taking over his room. At the end of the month, he does not have enough money to pay for his phone bill. He must sell some of his video games to keep his phone active. This happens for several months: Roger runs out of money and needs to sell games (for less than he paid) to pay his bills. A friend suggests that he should visit the library and borrow games instead of buying them. It is free to do so. This way, he can save money and keep his love of gaming satisfied. After taking his friend's advice, Roger finds he has plenty of money at the end of the month for bills.

✳ ✳ ✳

Juan likes to go to the movies every Saturday night. When he goes, he buys popcorn and a drink. The movie ticket is fifteen dollars. Popcorn and a drink cost eight dollars. He has only twenty dollars every week to spend and must figure out a way to save some money. Online, he sees that if he goes to a show before noon, tickets are only eight dollars. He decides to attend the early show so he has enough for the ticket and the snacks.

directions

1. Going back to your interest inventory, think about ways you spend your leisure time. Are there any ways you can save money? Can you find ways to engage in activities for free that still satisfy your interests?

Interest	How can you satisfy this interest with money?	How can you satisfy this interest without money?

2. Which activities have the best opportunities for free or reduced prices?

_____

_____

_____

take note

Developing a budget for your leisure can be easy. Let's fill out the form to see how much discretionary spending you have. Use the blank lines to add any other expenses not already mentioned. At http://www.newharbinger.com/40644, you can download a copy of this form.

What I need to pay for each month	How much I spend for these needs each month
Bills I must pay (include rent, phone, and any utilities)	
Daily living needs (food, toiletries, and any materials you need to use)	
Money I put away for savings each month	
Travel expenses	
Other:	
Other:	
Other:	

Add up the total amount of money needed each month $ _____

Subtract your total from the amount of your monthly allowance.

My monthly allowance $ _____

—

Total I spend on basic needs $ _____

Money left for leisure   = $ _____

Fill in the chart to see if you have enough money for your leisure activities.

Monthly amount for leisure   = $ _____

List the activities and how much you spend in a month in the chart below.

Leisure activity	Cost per month

Total spent per month on leisure activities   = $ _____

Do you have enough to satisfy your leisure time every month? If not, where can you cut back?

_____

_____

_____

online safety during leisure activities 29

you need to know

In activity 18, we touched on Internet safety. When it comes to leisure activities, it is important to revisit the issue of safe online practices. The Internet is full of ways to spend free time. Video games, social media like Instagram and Facebook, and blog posts are all ways of getting information and connecting with people. There are important rules to follow to keep your personal information safe as well as to protect yourself in situations where you are communicating with someone you do not know.

Wendy goes online to chat with friends. She begins to chat with someone who says she is female and the same age as Wendy and says her name is Sally. Sally repeatedly asks Wendy to meet her at her house. Sally says she has similar interests, and they would have a good time. Wendy knows she should not go, but she is curious. Having taken technology classes, Wendy knows that people often are not who they say they are online. Sally could be someone other than a female who is the same age. Sally could be someone who plans to harm or rob Wendy. There is no way of knowing. Wendy clearly tells Sally that she never meets people in person that she chats with online. Sally keeps on persisting, so Wendy blocks her from her chat site.

* * *

Roxanne has a website. She posts her interests about cooking. She shares recipes and tips for cooking. She puts lots of pictures of herself cooking and shopping on the website. Someone starts writing to her and making fun of her website. The person writing is very rude and uses improper language. Roxanne blocks the person from the website. Roxanne soon realizes that the person who was writing her was posting pictures of her on Facebook and other sites. The person is writing terrible things about Roxanne for no reason. Roxanne has to shut her site down and start over. She now does not share photos of herself, and she uses an alias. She tracks who is allowed to see the site and can block anyone from entering. After setting up these safety features, she is better prepared for securing her online presence.

directions

In each scenario, write what you would do to keep yourself and your personal information safe.

You're chatting on social media with someone who seems nice and wants to meet you in person. He tells you to come to his house. What do you do? Why?

_____

_____

_____

_____

In the above example, you do not really know this person. Going to his house would be dangerous. He may be setting you up for a robbery or even worse. Never accept an invitation from someone you do not know.

You meet someone through a friend on Facebook. He seems really nice, and you begin to chat with him. He asks you to send photos of you wearing a bathing suit. What do you do? Why?

_____

_____

_____

_____

Someone asking you for provocative photos may be interested in sexual trolling. It is inappropriate for anyone to ask for these types of photos. You should always consider blocking people if they ask for inappropriate photos.

Someone is writing about a mutual friend on social media. She is writing terrible things about this friend and sharing it with all of her contacts. What do you do? Why?

_____

_____

_____

_____

Cyberbullying is a serious issue in our community. In most situations, you can block a person or alert the authorities if it is serious enough. The person being slandered can also contact the site administrator and get that person blocked from using the social media.

Someone is bullying you on social media. The person is saying nasty things and threatening to fight with you. Do you respond? What do you do? Why?

_____

_____

_____

_____

Whether it happens to you or a friend, people who cyberbully should immediately be blocked. You may then contact authorities or the website directly to make a complaint.

Some friends want you to share pictures of yourself showing private body parts. They are asking you to post them online. What do you do? Why?

_____

_____

_____

_____

Posting anything online can result in the whole world seeing it. Even a text can end up on Facebook, Instagram, or other sites. Never send any materials of a sexual nature to someone.

take note

Do you know? Which answer would you choose in each of these situations? Circle the best answer.

1. You see that many strangers are commenting on your photos on Instagram. What should you do?

    a. Change your setting so that only friends can see your photos.

    b. Invite all these strangers to see your photos.

    c. Do nothing. It is safe to have strangers view your photos and comment online.

2. Your birthday is your password for all your accounts, including your online banking. Which statement best describes your use of this password?

    a. It is great because you won't forget it.

    b. It is not a good password because someone could easily find out your birthday and get into all your accounts.

    c. It doesn't matter because no one should be using your password.

3. You receive an email from a company you do not know. The email says to immediately download a file that is attached and that you owe money. You should:

    a. Open the file immediately and see what is going on!

    b. Call the police.

    c. Delete the email immediately without opening the attachment.

4. You receive a text from a bank saying your bank account is frozen. The text says you should send over your Social Security number right away. You should:

   a. Delete the text and ignore it.

   b. Send the Social Security number.

   c. Send the Social Security number and your address so they have all the information.

5. You are receiving messages from someone who wants to meet you. You don't know this person, but he seems friendly and says he is your age. You tell him no, but he keeps insisting and sends dozens of messages every day. You should:

   a. Give in and meet him. He could be a new friend.

   b. Block him from your social media sites.

   c. Block him and contact the site administrator via email or telephone to report the issue.

Answer Key:

Question 1–a: Change your setting so that only friends can see your photos. Keep all your settings on private and share your information only with people you know.

Question 2–b: It is not a good password to use because it is very easy for someone to find out your birthday and get into all your accounts. Using a complex group of letters, numbers, and symbols will create a password that won't be easy for someone to figure out. In addition, different accounts should have different passwords. This way, anyone who does steal your password won't be able to access another account. It is also a good idea to change your passwords from time to time.

Question 3–c: Delete the email immediately without opening the attachment. Never open something on the computer or on your smartphone if you don't know what it is. Many of those attachments contain viruses or programs that can steal personal information. If a company needs to send you a bill or other information, they can do it by mail or over the phone. Don't open anything if you don't know who it is from!

Question 4–a: Delete the text and ignore it. You should never send personal information over the Internet or through a text. In addition, a bank or financial institution would never email you for your Social Security number, password, or other personal information. Banks and other businesses are very careful to keep a client's information private. Therefore, if you get an email or a text asking for personal information, it is probably someone up to no good.

Question 5–c: Block him and contact the site administrator via email or telephone to report the issue. This is serious. Anyone contacting you to meet that you don't know can be very dangerous. You must block that person and also get in touch with the site administrator (you can find the information via the search bar or on the website). The person who is "trolling" could be dangerous and must be stopped. The site administrator can stop his account. Bottom line? *Never* accept any invitation from strangers on social media.

30 planning a leisure activity

you need to know

You have explored your interests, thought about ways to find resources to support these interests, and explored ways to engage in safe online leisure activities. Now let's put it all together and look at what goes into planning how to spend your leisure time. We will need to think about time, travel, budget, and safety as we plan to engage in an outing or activity.

Yalini wants to see a baseball game. She looks at the team's website to see when the next home game will happen. She looks up the date and time of the game. She looks up the prices of the tickets. Not wanting to go alone, she calls a few friends, who agree to meet her at the stadium. Next she must figure out how to get to and from the stadium. She decides to take a bus there and a car service home. She calculates how much she will need. When getting ready, she puts her keys and smartphone in her purse along with her money. She is ready for a fun day at the ballpark!

Pryce loves model trains. He builds them and collects replicas. He wants to visit a nearby transit museum. He looks up the hours it is open on the Internet and plans to go. He knows exactly which train to take to get to the museum. Pryce heads to the museum. When he gets there, he sees that there is an entrance fee. He does not have enough money to buy a ticket. Unfortunately, he is unable to visit the museum that day.

Yalini and Pryce both did a fair amount of planning for their outings. But Pryce forgot something. He did not check to see how much it cost to get into the museum. When planning a trip, you have to think of all the essentials. Time, money, transportation, and other details should be considered before going out for a day of leisure.

directions

What details will you need to know when going out or planning each of these leisure activities?

How will you prepare for a night at the movies?

_____

_____

_____

You are about to throw a birthday party for a friend. What steps do you need to take to get this party going?

_____

_____

_____

_____

There is a concert coming to your town. You want to go with a friend. What things need to be considered when getting tickets?

_____

_____

_____

take note

Now it's time to create an actual plan. Think about an upcoming event or activity you plan on attending. What details will you need to think about before you finalize your plans? Fill in the boxes on the right with these details. A blank form can be downloaded at http://www.newharbinger.com/40644.

What is the activity or event you will participate in?	
Is this something you will do alone or with friends? If with friends, how will you let them know about it?	
What transportation will you need?	
Is there a fee? Are there any other things you will need money for (snacks, extras)?	
What date will you go? What time? Is there a time schedule you will need to know?	
What other details might you need to know?	

Part 4

Community Use

Participating in your local community is a part of everyday life. Knowing how to access the resources in the community and staying active in the many offerings available in your local neighborhood will enhance your social life and help maintain your interests. In addition, it is essential that you know where to find services like medical centers, police stations, and others you may require at some point.

Being an active member of your community will give you the ability to gain new experiences and interact with new people and environments. Getting out and about will give you the opportunity to practice your social skills and your daily living skills.

It is important that you get out into the community. Staying in the house for too long can be limiting. While television and video games can be fun, they need to be balanced with experiences with other people. In addition, to be the most independent person you can be, you will need to do your own shopping, and make appointments with doctors, dentists, and caregivers. You will discover a freedom in making choices for yourself and being able to access the many opportunities your community can offer.

Safety is a concern in the community. Always be alert and make sure you know where you are going. Make sure to plan ahead for any issues that may come up. Within this part, you will practice planning that can make your day successful.

By preparing and practicing your community navigation skills, you will be able to lead a more independent life and benefit from the many wonderful experiences your community has to offer.

31 knowing your community

you need to know

Knowing your community is a big job. There may be hundreds of services, stores, parks, and other resources you will want to access. It is easy to get confused, so knowing the details of your community will be helpful. Getting out on a daily basis is important to lead the most independent life you can. To do so, you need to know what your community offers. By exploring your surroundings, you may find new and exciting opportunities that you can explore.

As Bridgette heads to the grocery store, she takes a new route. As she walks down the new street, she notices a library that she has not seen before. She hadn't even known that her small town had a library. She decides to visit and learns about many programs offered, such as computer classes and book clubs—and all for free. Finding this new resource gives her new opportunities to try. Because she is very interested in technology, she signs up for one of the classes.

Catherine wants to have her hair done at a salon but is unsure about where to go. She uses Google Maps to find a salon near her house. She puts in her address and does a search for salons. She finds several and looks at the reviews under each salon. She decides on one and calls to make an appointment.

directions

Using Google Maps is a way to find local businesses and services you may want to use. Let's try to find some things that are in your community by following the steps below and looking at some options.

1. On a computer, go to the Google Maps website. In the upper left corner, type in your address.

2. Click on the small photo or address that pops up on the left side of the screen.

3. You will see a larger map of your area with many local businesses listed. Jot down a few of these that you know or would like to visit.

Name of business _____

Type of business _____

Name of business _____

Type of business _____

Name of business _____

Type of business _____

Name of business _____

Type of business _____

Name of business _____

Type of business _____

4. Click the button "Nearby" on the left side of the screen. Then press "Restaurants." You will see a list of restaurants that may be of interest. Choose one and list it here:

_____

5. The screen will show where this restaurant is. Next, click on "Directions" and type in your address again on the top line. The icons at the very top will show the transportation options, such as walking, driving, bicycling, or public transportation. Choose one.

_____

6. How far is it to your destination? How long will it take to get there?

_____

take note

Use Google Maps to find the following services. Write in any other services you might use. Note the distance, method of travel, and time it will take to get there.

Service	Address	Distance	How would I get there?	How long will it take to get there?
Supermarket				
Library				
Dentist's office				
Medical service				
Post office				
Restaurant				
Other services				
Other services				

32 supportive, social, and other essential resources in your community

you need to know

Resources in your community go beyond basic services like police, fire, and medical. They can include services that will help you in very specific ways. In many cases, these services include support geared at helping adults live independently. Services for people with autism are also available and can make a big difference in your life. There are many agencies and organizations that will support you and your specific needs.

George was having trouble at his job. He was frequently reprimanded by his supervisor for being impatient with customers. George had difficulty with outbursts and becoming easily upset. George had worked with an agency for adults with autism in the past and decided to call and see if they could help him with his issues at work. The agency was glad to help and offered George social skills classes. In addition, the agency worked with George at his job site to assist in job coaching. As a result, George's performance at work improved.

Every few months, the agency would check in with George's employer to make sure George was doing well at work. George continued to go to social skills classes, which helped him control his temper and find alternative ways of dealing with frustration. George also was able to take part in many other agency-sponsored events, such as dances, classes, and social outings.

directions

Below is a list of resources your community may offer. Use the Internet to see if there are any local offices in your area. Explore the services they offer and see if they are of interest or could provide you with some support. If these specific resources are not available, use a Google search to see if other agencies are available in your local community. Many of these agencies offer online support and services as well.

- Autismspeaks.org

  Click "Families & Adults"

  Click "Find Resources in Your Area"

  Choose the state you live in

- Nationalautismcenter.org

  Use the form to fill in your personal information. You will receive an email containing local resources for support.

- Easterseals.com

  Click "What We Do"

  Click "Young Adults"

  Look through the services available

- Nationalautismassociation.org

  Click "Local Resources"

  See if your state is included

- Autism-society.org

  A phone number is provided at the bottom of the page to help find local resources.

  Scroll down and click "AutismSource Database" for more information.

take note

What agencies offer support in your local area?

_____

_____

_____

What services do these agencies offer that may be of interest to you?

_____

_____

_____

Are there other local agencies you have used?

_____

_____

_____

What services do they offer?

_____

_____

_____

you need to know

It isn't enough to know where community resources are; it is also important to know what they offer that you can access. For every community resource you find, you need to ask a series of questions about the service they offer in order to help you use your time efficiently. By asking these questions you will be able to get as much information as you can to ensure you get what you need.

Alice wanted to visit a local art gallery. She looked up the times and dates it was open. She checked about the fee for entering. She looked up the address on the Internet and found she could easily get there using a public bus. Upon arriving at the gallery, she realized she was unable to enter. The gallery did not have an American with Disabilities Act–approved ramp. Alice used a wheelchair, and the set of stairs was not accessible for her.

* * *

Carrie wanted to do her grocery shopping and located a few grocery store options. She was a vegetarian and wanted to find a store that had a wide selection of vegetarian products. She called each of the grocery stores and asked about their products. One store did have a wide range of vegetarian products; the others did not. Carrie was able to find what she needed by making the phone call.

directions

What questions do these people need to ask in order to make sure they can access the community resource?

Roger needs to stop by the grocery store after work. He is not sure if the store will be open. He calls the store. What should he ask?

_____

_____

Elisa needs a dentist. She needs to use her insurance for this visit because she cannot pay out of pocket. She calls a local dentist for an appointment. What should she ask?

_____

_____

David wants to find a local gym. His favorite form of exercise is swimming. What should he ask the gym?

_____

_____

Karen needs to find a new bank. She doesn't have a lot of money and does not want to pay any fees for opening a new account. What would she ask a new bank?

_____

_____

Ananth uses a wheelchair. He is interested in seeing a movie at the local theater. Before going, what should he ask the theater?

_____

_____

take note

If you need special attention in any of the areas below, write down what you should ask when trying to access a local service.

Dietary needs

_____

_____

_____

_____

Banking needs

_____

_____

_____

_____

Physical needs

_____

_____

_____

_____

What type of medical insurance do you have? Do you have doctors who take that insurance?

_____

_____

_____

_____

don't let others take advantage of you 34

you need to know

Using the resources in your community means traveling to and from places safely and interacting with many people. Wherever you go, making sure others do not take advantage of you is something to always keep in your mind. Unfortunately, there are times people may try to take advantage of you by charging you more for something or not delivering on a promise. People on the street may ask you for money. In some cases, people can be lured into situations that are dangerous. You must stay sharp and follow your plans without distraction. While there are many laws protecting people with disabilities, people can often take advantage of someone who is not aware.

Kofi leaves his apartment and looks for a taxi to take him to his cousin's house. He usually finds a licensed cab to take him. A black car stops, and the driver asks him if he needs a cab. Kofi says yes and gets in. This cab is not licensed, and the driver charges Kofi twice what a regular cab does.

✳ ✳ ✳

Julia is approached by a stranger who says he can offer her a job that pays a lot of money. She only needs to pose for some photos. Julia immediately walks away because she knows that this person is probably up to no good and will use the photos for illicit purposes.

✳ ✳ ✳

Carla is crossing the street. A man starts screaming at her for money. She has no idea who he is and becomes frightened. She empties her wallet, giving the stranger her money, and runs away. When she gets home, her sister tells her she should not have given him any money and instead called for help.

159

directions

Answer these questions, keeping in mind the best practices to follow when traveling.

A stranger asks for money. You know you should never give money to strangers. What do you do?

_____

_____

_____

When traveling, why should you not accept rides from strangers?

_____

_____

_____

Do you use Uber or another app to access a car service? When using a car service, what things should you keep in mind?

_____

_____

_____

Why should you never get into a car you did not call for?

_____

_____

_____

People on the street may approach you with questions or offers that make you uncomfortable. What would you do if someone who started talking to you on the street made you feel uncomfortable?

_____

_____

_____

take note

Being taken advantage of puts you in a situation that could cause you bodily harm or financial loss. If you ever feel threatened or taken advantage of, get help immediately. Think about the following:

- Is someone threatening to hurt you physically?

- Is someone hurting you physically?

- Is someone touching you in a sexual way that is uninvited?

- Is someone withholding food, or any basic necessity, from you?

- Is someone taking money from you without permission?

- Are you being paid what you should be at work?

- Is anyone intentionally harming you? Demeaning or insulting to you?

- Is anyone causing you fear?

If any of these things were applicable to you now or in the future, who would you go to for help (for example, family members, police, friends)?

_____

_____

_____

_____

you need to know

When running errands, you need to think about a few things. Are you able to wait in line patiently? What happens when a store or service is not available? How do you interact with employees? Do you know where your local services (for example, post offices or libraries) are? You also need to know the hours of the places you are going before you go so you don't waste a trip. Running errands is an important part of becoming independent; the more you can do by yourself, the more options in your life you will have.

Elizabeth needs to buy cat food at the pet store, pick up her laundry, stop at the pharmacy for her prescription, and buy stamps at the post office. Knowing that her laundry will be a little heavy, she decides to go there last so she won't have to lug her bag all over town. For the remaining errands, she will first complete the one that is farthest from home. She starts by taking the bus to the pet store. After the pet store, she walks to the post office, which is close. She then takes the bus back to the pharmacy. Her prescription is not ready, and she still needs to pick up her laundry. She calls the laundromat to see when they close. She realizes that she has enough time to wait for her prescription and then walk over to the laundromat. She will take a cab home so she doesn't have to carry her laundry bag home.

Upon arriving home, Elizabeth realizes that she has completed all her errands successfully. Even though there were a lot of steps, she successfully navigated the travel and sequencing necessary to finish everything.

directions

What can the person in each scenario do to make sure he completes the errand successfully?

Robert has enough money to pay for two of three items he needs from the drugstore. One solution would be to prioritize the items. What would he need to think about to do so? What should he do?

_____

_____

_____

Another solution could be to put it on a charge card. What would he need to think about in this case?

_____

_____

When picking up his prescription, Jeff always has to wait at least thirty minutes. What should he bring with him to help pass the time?

_____

_____

_____

Alfred needs to get his cell phone fixed. He looks for local businesses that provide the service. He finds four nearby. What should he think about when deciding which to visit?

_____

_____

_____

take note

What errands do you run regularly? What do you need to think about for each that will help you be successful? What could you do to help each errand go more smoothly?

Errand	What do you need to think about?	What would make it go more smoothly?

36 interacting with community workers

you need to know

Interacting with community workers like doctors, store clerks, and other individuals will help you access the resources you need if you are clear, concise, and polite. In addition, being specific about your needs will help you get what you want in an efficient manner. When interacting with anyone in the community to access a need, it is important to make a good impression. Becoming agitated or upset when you don't get the help you need will complicate a situation.

Harry needed to buy shampoo, but the brand he used was not in stock. He became nervous about not getting what he needed and angrily asked the clerk in the store where his shampoo was. The clerk was confused and didn't understand the request. Harry became more and more agitated and began to raise his voice. The manager of the store escorted Harry out the door and asked him not to come back.

✳ ✳ ✳

Frank needed to buy shampoo, but the brand he used was not in stock. He became nervous about not finding what he needed. He politely asked the clerk to help him find the brand he needed. The clerk checked the shelf and told Frank that the brand he wanted was out of stock. He recommended a brand that was very similar to the one Frank used. Frank thanked the clerk and made his purchase. By being flexible, he got what he needed.

directions

Using clear, concise, and polite language, write the question you would ask each of these community workers.

1. You are trying to fill your train pass with money. The machine you are using is not working. Who should you find to help you? What do you ask?

   _____

   _____

   _____

2. You go to the hardware store for a specific size screw, but there are so many! You have no idea which one would be correct. Who do you ask for help? What do you say?

   _____

   _____

   _____

3. At a restaurant, the waiter brings you the wrong meal. Who should you speak with? What do you say?

   _____

   _____

   _____

4. At the market, you cannot find the fruit section. You look everywhere but just don't see it. You ask a clerk who tells you where to go, but when you get there, there is no fruit section. You are getting annoyed. What do you do? What do you ask?

_____

_____

_____

take note

Write about an experience with a community worker when you needed help.

_____

_____

_____

How did it feel to ask for help?

_____

_____

_____

Was there a time you were not able to access help? If that happens again, what could you do differently?

_____

_____

_____

_____

_____

Looking ahead, when might be the next time you will need to access help? How can you prepare yourself?

_____

_____

_____

_____

_____

37 what to take with you

---

you need to know

Planning ahead is the most important thing to do when getting ready for a community outing. What to take with you when you leave in the morning or are heading to an event is an important part of this planning. Nothing feels worse than getting to a show and realizing you forgot the tickets.

You can easily avoid problems using a checklist. Try to stay a step ahead by thinking about where you are going and what you will need.

Jeanie planned a trip to the library. She would return books, take out new ones, and spend some time doing research on the computer. She sat down and wrote a list of what she would need when she got to the library. She included her cell phone, her bus pass, books she needed to return, house keys, and a bottle of water. She went to the library the next day and did everything she needed to get done. It was a successful trip.

✳ ✳ ✳

David carries his book bag everywhere. It contains books, games, papers, and lots of things he doesn't need. One morning at his local art class, he needed to take some work home. Unfortunately, his book bag was so full that he had to force the work into his bag. When he got home, his work was crumpled.

✳ ✳ ✳

Cara hurries out of the house to meet friends at a diner for lunch. Cara is running late and unfortunately forgets her wallet. A friend lends her money, but Cara feels embarrassed.

directions

You have learned in past activities about being prepared—making sure you have the things you need for specific community events. But there are also things that may be unforeseen when you are going out for the day. Think about what you may need in addition to the obvious to have a successful event.

Your day group is taking a bus to the beach. It is a long ride. You have your swimsuit, towel, suntan lotion, sunglasses, and cell phone. It is a long ride, and no food or water will be available for purchase. What else might you bring?

_____

_____

You have a doctor's appointment. When you go to this office, you usually wait about an hour. You have all your updated paperwork, insurance card, and other important documents. What might you bring to pass the time while you have to wait?

_____

_____

You are going out to dinner with friends. You need to take medication at 7:00 p.m. Dinner is at 6:00 p.m. You also are not sure how much this dinner will cost. What do you bring with you to ensure that you have a great evening?

_____

_____

take note

What do you need when you are going out in the community? Of course, the answer depends on where you are going. But let's think about what you may need on your daily routines and then think about what you should add in case circumstances change.

Where are you going?	What do you take?	What else should you bring in case …
To work		… you need to work late?
Name an event you attend:		… there are transportation difficulties?
Name a leisure activity:		… the site ie closed when you get there?
Name an educational activity you attend:		… your class wants to go out afterward?

you need to know

What do you wear? Who do you need to contact? Will you be back for your next appointment? It is great to get out into the community, but there are many things to think about before you go. Things as simple as checking the weather can make your community experience much better. You need to think of other things that may affect your trip. Checking the weather, possible transportation delays, and your daily schedule are the first steps.

Jill is ready to go out on her daily errands. Before she leaves, she turns on the television to catch the weather report. She hears that there is a good chance of rain. She packs an umbrella in her bag. Sure enough, it starts to rain while she is out, but she is well prepared.

* * *

Wendy rides the same bus to work every day. One morning, she waits for the bus longer than usual. The bus finally arrives, but Wendy is going to be late to work. When she gets there, a coworker tells her that the buses are running late due to construction. Her coworker has an app that alerts her to any transit issues. Wendy downloads the app and is ready the next time there is a problem with the bus system.

* * *

At noon every day, Max takes a certain medication. One day he has back-to-back appointments with the dentist and a job coach. He plans for the outing and makes a list of everything he will need. He will be gone from 8:00 a.m. to 3:00 p.m. Fortunately, his roommate reminds him that he has to take medication at noon, and he won't be home to do so. Max puts his medication into a ziplock bag. This way, he won't miss his daily dosage.

directions

Each scenario includes something these people did not plan for. What action should they have taken before they left for their community outing?

Walter is walking between the gym and his doctor's appointment. It starts to rain. What should he have done before leaving the house?

_____

Abel is on his way to look at an apartment for rent. When he gets to the address, he is not sure which apartment he should look at. He wants to call the broker but does not know the number. What should he have done before leaving?

_____

Ricki is at the movies. She is having a great time. When she gets home, she receives a call asking where she was at 2:00 p.m., as she had an interview scheduled at that time. Before leaving for the movies, what should she have done?

_____

Paola left for her weekly shopping trip. She walked to the supermarket. She has everything she needed: wallet, cell phone, and grocery list. At the checkout counter, her credit card is declined. Apparently she had forgotten to pay the bill. What might she have done to avoid this situation?

_____

Michael is going to do some errands, and he is going to take his car. He has everything he needs for the day. On his way, the car stops running. It has run out of gas! What should Michael have done before leaving?

_____

take note

What to think about before an outing includes thinking about things that may not seem obvious. While it is hard to predict every possible circumstance, there are some things you can do every time you are on your way out to avoid problems.

For example, why is it a good idea to check the weather before leaving the house?

_____

_____

_____

Why should you check the news for travel information or check your public transportation app before setting out on a trip?

_____

_____

_____

Why should you check your bank account or credit card statement before going out and spending money?

_____

_____

_____

Why should you look at your daily planner or schedule before leaving for the day?

_____

_____

_____

Write down other things to think about before leaving home for your errand or outing.

_____

_____

_____

you need to know

It is time to put together all you know about the resources in your community and plan a trip. We have used checklists and charts to help us plan for things throughout these activities. Let's see how they can help us now.

As the weekend approaches, Gene is planning for a trip to the beach. He will need to pack supplies for the day, as well as figure out how to get to the beach. He knows that there is a train that stops close to the beach and that he will have to take a bus the rest of the way. He will begin to plan by looking up the train and bus schedules for going to and coming home from the beach and finding out the ticket prices for both the bus and the train.

Because he is going to be out for a good part of the day, he will need to pack a few things. What should he take? He packs a swimsuit, towel, sunscreen, hat, blanket, and sunglasses. He has a waterproof pouch for his cell phone and wallet. He will need to bring food and water.

Gene makes a list so that on the day of his trip he is ready to go. He thinks that it may be more fun if he invites some friends. He calls a few people who are also excited to go to the beach. He shares his list so that they too will be prepared for what is sure to be a fun day.

directions

Time to plan an outing. If you were going for a checkup, how would you plan to ensure a successful trip to the doctor's office? Let's use the chart to help you remember everything you will need. At http://www.newharbinger.com/40644, you can download a blank copy of this chart.

Where are you going: You are going to the doctor's for a checkup.
What will you need to bring with you?
How will you get there? How will you get home?
When is this appointment? Check your calendar to see if there is anything you may need to arrange in your schedule.
Are there other things to consider? Are you going alone? Should you let someone know where you are going?

take note

Think about an upcoming community outing. Where are you going, and what is the purpose?

_____

_____

_____

How would you locate where you want to go? What is the address?

_____

_____

_____

List the things you will need to bring with you.

- _____
- _____
- _____
- _____
- _____
- _____
- _____
- _____

Is this something you will do alone? Can you invite friends?

_____

_____

What other things should you think about before you leave?

_____

_____

_____

problem solving when things go wrong 40

you need to know

Despite the best planning, there are going to be times when things go wrong. The most important thing is to stay calm and think about solutions to the problem. If something does go wrong, it doesn't mean the day is ruined. Sometimes a simple solution is all it takes to get back on track.

Todd is traveling with his group on a trip to the museum. They are traveling on the subway. By mistake, Todd exits the train at the wrong stop. His group is still on the train. At first, Todd becomes extremely nervous. He is alone and not very familiar with the train system. Fortunately, his group leader prepared him for this situation. He remembers the leader telling him that if he ever gets separated from the group, he should wait at the station and someone would return. Todd waits. He is still a bit nervous, but knows it may take a little while before someone returns for him. Sure enough, in about ten minutes one of the group workers meets him at the station. They wait for the next train and soon are back with the group.

directions

Think about each situation. In each, the first step is to remain calm. Think about a good solution to each problem.

At a restaurant with his friend, Kyle realizes he forgot his wallet. What should he do?

_____

_____

_____

Jason is at the museum with his group. When he looks around, he realizes he is separated from his group. What should he do?

_____

_____

_____

John needs to call his job to tell his boss that he will be late. He is at the bus stop. Unfortunately, his phone is not charged. What should he do?

_____

_____

_____

Wilfredo needs to pick up his cleaning. He looks for his ticket. Despite searching everywhere, he cannot find it. What should he do?

_____

_____

_____

Edie is going to her sister's house. When she gets to the station, she sees a sign that says the train will be late. She is nervous because her sister is waiting to pick Edie up from the station. What should she do?

_____

_____

_____

take note

Being prepared is key to finding a solution to a problem. Take a moment to reflect on situations that may have needed problem solving. Use moments from your life that either went well or didn't go well. Reflect on how it could have gone better.

Situation	Your solution	How did things work out?	What might you have done differently?

Francis Tabone, PhD, is head of the Cooke Center for Learning and Development. He has been both a teacher and administrator for the Department of Education in New York, NY, developing innovative programming for special-needs students. Tabone serves as adjunct professor of special education at several colleges and universities. He resides in New York, NY.

Foreword writer **Judith Newman** is author of *To Siri With Love*, a collection of illuminating stories about life with an autistic son. In addition to books and personal essays, Newman writes for magazines about entertainment, science, business, beauty, health, and popular culture. Her work has been featured in a variety of publications. Newman, her husband, and their twin sons reside in New York, NY.

More ⏱ Instant Help Books for Teens

An Imprint of New Harbinger Publications

**THE AUTISM PLAYBOOK
FOR TEENS**

Imagination-Based Mindfulness
Activities to Calm Yourself,
Build Independence &
Connect with Others

978-1626250093 / US $16.95

**THINK CONFIDENT,
BE CONFIDENT FOR TEENS**

A Cognitive Therapy Guide to
Overcoming Self-Doubt & Creating
Unshakable Self-Esteem

978-1608821136 / US $16.95

**A TEEN'S GUIDE TO
GETTING STUFF DONE**

Discover Your Procrastination
Type, Stop Putting Things Off
& Reach Your Goals

978-1626255876 / US $16.95

**COMMUNICATION SKILLS
FOR TEENS**

How to Listen, Express
& Connect for Success

978-1626252639 / US $16.95

**THE EXECUTIVE
FUNCTIONING WORKBOOK
FOR TEENS**

Help for Unprepared, Late
& Scattered Teens

978-1608826568 / US $17.95

**THE SOCIAL SUCCESS
WORKBOOK FOR TEENS**

Skill-Building Activities for Teens
with Nonverbal Learning Disorder,
Asperger's Disorder & Other
Social-Skill Problems

978-1572246140 / US $15.95

newharbingerpublications
1-800-748-6273 / newharbinger.com

(VISA, MC, AMEX / prices subject to change without notice)

Follow Us 🅕 🅣 🅞 🅟

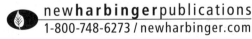

Don't miss out on new books in the subjects that interest you.
Sign up for our **Book Alerts** at **newharbinger.com/bookalerts**

Register your **new harbinger** titles for additional benefits!

When you register your **new harbinger** title—purchased in any format, from any source—you get access to benefits like the following:

- Downloadable accessories like printable worksheets and extra content

- Instructional videos and audio files

- Information about updates, corrections, and new editions

Not every title has accessories, but we're adding new material all the time.

Access free accessories in 3 easy steps:

1. Sign in at NewHarbinger.com (or **register** to create an account).

2. Click on **register a book**. Search for your title and click the **register** button when it appears.

3. Click on the **book cover or title** to go to its details page. Click on **accessories** to view and access files.

That's all there is to it!

If you need help, visit:

NewHarbinger.com/accessories

new harbinger
CELEBRATING
40 YEARS